COLONIAL
DELAWARE
RECORDS

1681-1713

BRUCE A. BENDLER

HERITAGE BOOKS
2008

HERITAGE BOOKS
AN IMPRINT OF HERITAGE BOOKS, INC.

Books, CDs, and more—Worldwide

For our listing of thousands of titles see our website
at
www.HeritageBooks.com

Published 2008 by
HERITAGE BOOKS, INC.
Publishing Division
100 Railroad Ave. #104
Westminster, Maryland 21157

Other books by the author:
Colonial Delaware Assemblymen 1682-1776

International Standard Book Numbers
Paperbound: 978-1-58549-214-5
Clothbound: 978-0-7884-7083-7

CONTENTS

Preface v

Introduction vii

Kent County Rent Roll, 1681 - 1688 1

Sussex County Rent Roll, 1681 - 1688 7

1693 Tax Assessment List of New Castle County 10

1693 Tax Assessment List of Kent County 20

1693 Tax Assessment List of Sussex County 26

Kent County, Quitrents, c. 1701 - 1713 30

Sussex County Quitrents, 1702 - 1713 45

Index 63

PREFACE

The records of early Delaware are to be found in a number of repositories. Because of the proprietorship of the Penn family over the Three Lower Counties, a number of these records can be found in the Penn papers and those of his political associates, many of which are located in the collections of the Historical Society of Pennsylvania in Philadelphia. In the course of my own historical and genealogical research, I found the papers published herein to be of particular value. These include a tax list of 1693, which is among the Three Lower Counties Papers. Quitrents for Kent and Sussex Counties for the early eighteenth century are found in Book 16 of the Logan Papers. A Rent Roll encompassing the 1680's is included in Volume One of Penn's accounts.

I gratefully acknowledge the permission of the Historical Society of Pennsylvania to publish these items. It is my hope that the reader will find them as useful a resource as I have. Finally, I would like to dedicate this work to the memory of Raymond B. Clark, Jr., whose role in my own development as an historian and genealogist cannot be quantified.

Bruce A. Bendler
Bear, Delaware
February, 1992

INTRODUCTION

In 1682, William Penn became proprietor of the three counties which now comprise the state of Delaware. Before that year, Delaware had been under the dominion of the Swedes, the Dutch, and the Duke of York, brother of King Charles II of England. Penn obtained what came to be known as the Three Lower Counties on Delaware by a grant from the Duke of York, who became James II upon his brother's death. Because of these many changes of government, records of Delaware are to be found in many different repositories. Many of these records have been published, however. Information about the Swedes can be found in the work of Amandus Johnson.[1] The papers edited by Charles T. Gehring are the best source for the period of Dutch rule and that of the Duke of York.[2] Other Dutch records have been published in *Delaware History*, the journal of the Historical Society of Delaware.[3] Land grants during the rule of the Dutch and the Duke of York were published by the General Assembly of Delaware.[4]

The records of Delaware from the early years of William Penn's rule are even more widely scattered. Some of them remained in the private papers of Penn and his close associates, and are now among the collections of the Historical Society of Pennsylvania in Philadelphia. It is from these papers that the records in this work have been taken.

The rent rolls of the 1680's list the landowner, the dates on which the land was granted and surveyed, and the name, if any, given to the property. The rent rolls were located in Volume 16 of the Logan papers. The tax list of 1693 is part of a collection known as the Three Lower Counties Papers, documents relating specifi-

1   Amandus Johnson, *Swedish Settlements on the Delaware 1638-1664*, 2 vol., (Burt Franklin, New York, 1969 repr.).

2   Charles T. Gehring, ed., *New York Historical Manuscripts: Dutch (English Period, Delaware Papers)*, Vols. XX and XXI, (Genealogical Publishing Company, Baltimore, 1977).

3   C. A. Weslager, "The City of Amsterdam's Colony on the Delaware, 1656-1664; With Unpublished Dutch Notorial Abstracts," *Delaware History XX*, (Wilmington, 1982).

4   *The Duke of York Records*, (Sunday Star Print, Wilmington, 1903), repr. by Family Line Publications, Westminster, 1989.

cally to colonial Delaware. The quitrents form part of the accounts papers of the Penn family. They trace the titles for properties for which the rents were disputed; many times the title is traced to the original owner of the property. Thus, data valuable to both historians and genealogists are provided.

The process of acquiring land from the proprietor is described by Dr. John A. Munroe:

> "From the secretary of the Land Office, normally also the provincial secretary, a warrant had first to be secured by anyone desiring to establish title to a tract of new land. The warrant was an order for a survey, which could be made by the surveyor general or, more likely, by a deputy. In general, the applicant could pick out any parcel of unsurveyed land he pleased, of any shape, as long as Indian title had been cleared and no prior title or survey had been taken to it. He was expected to choose a moderate quantity, which in most cases meant two hundred or three hundred acres, and when he paid for the land a patent was issued which was his deed or title."[1]

Quitrents were generally low, either a penny per acre, or a bushel of wheat per one hundred acres.[2] Efforts to collect the rents met with mixed success.

The late seventeenth and early eighteenth centuries are times for which genealogical research in Delaware is especially difficult. Locating records is a major factor in the difficulty involved. This book is an attempt to present some of the records which the author believes will be especially helpful to researchers.

---

1   John A. Munroe, *Colonial Delaware: A History*, (KTO Press, Millwood, N. Y., 1978), p. 217.

2   *Ibid.*, pp. 93, 217.

KENT COUNTY RENT ROLL, 1681-1688

Owner	Tract Name	Acres	Surveyed	Granted
William Allen	Rochester	500	20-12-83	15-6-82
Jno Alburton &	Maydston	870	6-9-84	19-2-81
Jno Mumford	Topsham	353	7-9-84	19-2-81
John Alford	Alburne	1200	23-9-85	15-1-81
Peter Bawcomb	Arundell	880	3-11-83	15-1-81
Peter Bawcomb	Shearness	220	20-11-88	17-9-80
John Burton	Chance	100	21-4-84	21-10-82
Jane Bartlet	Poplar Ridge	380	8-9-84	21-10-80
John Burton	The Triangle	300	6-9-84	21-10-80
Nich Bartlet	Longacre	1000	16-12-85	21-1-82
Rich Bartlet	Bartlets lot	1150	1-9-87	
Saml Burbery				
Jno Bedwell				
Frederick Phillips				
Saml Burbery		130		
John Brooks	Edmunds Berry	1000	23-1-85	15-1-81
Richard Bayley	Middleborough	1200	16-12-85	15-1-81
Henry Bishop	Rodney Stock	800	19-3-86	21-12-81
Benony Bishop	St. Cullomb	1400	21-4-85	20-10-81
Robert Bedwell	The Flowery Neck	1050	21-6-85	20-6-79
Michael Bosne	Lambourne	500	21-9-85	20-10-80
John Brinklow	Lisbon	750	5-11-85	21-4-81
John Brinklow	Brinklow's Gift	575	6-12-85	21-4-81
John Brinklow		1000	25-11-85	21-12-81
John Betts	Middletowne	1000	25-2-85	21-12-81
Henry Bowman	Sawmill Range	2000	1-1-86	
John Bradshaw	Golden Ridge	300	24-4-84	15-1-81
John Bradshaw	Bradshaw's Berry	160	3-12-84	15-1-81
Josh Barkstead		300	3-10-86	
Daniell Browne		300	21-12-84	15-9-81
Daniell Browne		900		
John Barnes			22-11-83	21-4-82

1

Tho Bostock		600	11-10-86	15-6-82
John Biggs		300	22-11-79	1-1-84
Norton Claypoole	Greenwich	1000	20-4-84	21-12-81
George Clifford	Smirna	600	20-4-84	17-8-82
Tho Clifford	Shipton	300	17-11-83	21-3-82
Alexander Chance	Davids Berry	300	15-10-85	15-6-82
Alexander Chance	Elks Horne	85	21-6-85	15-6-82
Samuel Cooper	Coopersbury	400	15-12-85	15-6-82
Samuel Cooper	(now John Mills)	400	22-11-87	
John Cropper	Springfield	1000	20-12-85	15-9-82
James Cooper	Coopers Hall	300	10-7-84	21-12-81
John Curtis	Swampbourne	160	11-9-87	21-12-81
John Curtis	Pasture Point	50	18-8-87	2-12-81
John Curtis	Stratham	600	19-8-87	
John Curtis	Point Lookout	300	19-2-84	21-12-81
George Cullen	Angleton	400	22-12-85	15-1-81
John Courtney	Burberrys Berry	400	21-11-83	23-11-82
William Clark		412	13-11-80	26-1-84
John Davis &	Flowerfield	1200	20-9-85	15-10-80
Thos Flower				
Wm Dervall &	Fairfield	2000	18-11-85	20-10-81
Wm Clark				
Will Dervall		1200	10-11-83	21-1-82
Alexander Draper	Drapersbury	1000	6-12-85	21-12-81
William Dickson		600	21-12-85	20-4-82
Danl Dempsey	Barkinton	600	18-3-86	17-8-81
Wm Darrington		600	13-11-83	21-1-82
Jno Edmunson	Micheltowne	300	21-12-85	
William Emmat	Wheatfield	1000	28-12-85	20-10-81
William Ellinsworth		1025	2-1-85	21-2-82
William Freeman	Freemans Range	600	14-12-85	21-12-81
William Framton	Whitwells	1374	-85	7-4-86
Widow Framton	Bear Garden	800	24-2-87	
Elizabeth Framton		470	23-2-87	
Elizabeth Framton		700	23-12-86	

Edward Fredrick	The Vineyard	400	6-12-84	
Robert Francis	Point Lookout	200	18-9-80	15-9-81
William Framton		1000	10-11-83	10-4-84
William Framton		1000	26-11-83	29-5-84
John Glover	Teyneds Court	93	5-8-83	21-10-80
John & Rich Glover		1200	15-11-83	21-10-80
Peter Gronendik	Sittingburn	420	22-12-83	21-12-81
Peter Gronendik	Goosberry	600	20-12-85	21-10-80
for Cornelius Verhoof				
Edmd Gibbon	Tidbury	400	16-10-84	
Edmd Gibbon	Tenderith	1000	20-11-84	20-10-81
Francis Gibbon	Lusham	1000	10-11-84	20-10-81
Tho Grove &	Woodford	900	7-12-85	15-10-81
Jno Walker				
Thomas Grove	Kneckinton	300	7-9-87	21-7-81
Joseph Growdon	Rinier	650	27-1-88	16-2-86
more to him		1000	17-1-88	16-2-86
Patrick Grady	Gradington	500	12-12-85	15-6-82
Robert Gillom	Anglefield	450	5-12-85	21-7-81
William Greene		1050	12-9-83	21-7-81
Alexander Humfry	Greenway	600	28-7-83	21-1-82
Alexr Humfry		1000	25-11-82	21-12-81
Alexr Humfry	Brocknock	600	8-11-84	17-9-80
Thomas Heatherd	Ausbog	1600	9-9-83	15-6-82
Thomas Heather	Ingleborough	200	1-2-85	15-6-82
John Hilliard	Hillington	300	19-9-85	15-1-81
John Hilliard	Hilton	1200	24-9-85	15-1-81
John Hilliard	Whitehall	600	14-2-87	15-4-73
John Hilliard	Hilburne	700	26-2-87	15-1-81
John Hilliard	Partnership	800	6-1-84	7-3-83
Charles Hilliard	Mother Plantation	200	15-2-87	19-1-74
Thomas Hilliard		100	16-2-87	19-4-71
Oliver Hilliard		100	17-2-87	19-4-71
Richard Holland	Holland	1200	26-9-85	
George Horfford	Barron Point	1000	4-12-85	26-10-81

3

Barnet Hodges	James Valley	500	5-3-78	
John Hill	Hill's Adventure	800	1-10-81	21-10-81
Thomas Hill	Seaton	600	7-20-86	
William Hill		180	22-2-87	
Robert Hudson		800	27-9-83	21-10-80
John Hoggister	Mount(?)	600	20-12-84	15-1-81
Thomas Hassold	Improvement	150	15-9-83	21-1-82
Thomas Jarvis	Barkstead Hazzard	300	10-5-85	17-9-80
Simon Irons	Irons Addition	232	21-10-85	20-4-82
Simon Irons		1000	10-9-86	20-4-82
Simon Irons		610	10-9-86	20-4-82
Evan Jones	Appaconie	300	28-10-85	21-7-80
Evan Jones	High Cross	470	29-9-86	21-4-81
Evan Jones		470	4-9-86	
Daniell James		600	20-12-85	14-3-87
John Kelly	Killington	570	23-2-84	20-10-81
John King		1200	13-10-83	17-10-82
& Robert Betts				
Richard Levick	Edington	320	9-3-83	17-9-80
Hugh Luft	Manloes Bounds	100	10-4-86	
Hugh Luft		100	10-4-86	
Charles Murphy	Gravesend	600	14-12-83	21-1-82
George Martin	Woodstock Corner	1500	23-5-85	24-12-84
George Martin	Bradshaws Choice	270	29-12-83	21-10-80
George Martin	Price's Choice	100	27-10-85	
George Martin	James' Choice	100	27-10-85	
George Martin		200	20-9-87	
John Manlow	Improvement	600	23-11-85	26-8-82
John Manlow	Clayton	200	2-12-85	21-1-82
Samuel Mott	Motlow	400	7-12-85	20-10-81
John Manlow	Manslow	400	3-12-85	21-10-80
Joseph Moore	Greenfield	600	26-12-83	19-9-81
Christopher Moore		400	29-9-83	17-3-82
James Maxfield		50	5-2-88	
John Mills		32	10-4-87	

4

John Mills vide. Sam Cooper		400		
John Newall	The Reserve	400	28-7-83	21-7-80
Edward Newton	Newington	500	25-9-85	21-10-80
Richard Noble	Rich Pasture	1000	12-2-87	20-10-80
Bapts Newcomb		600	20-9-84	10-2-85
Brian O'Neale	The Downes	400	23-11-83	21-12-81
Edward Packe	Kingston	180	1-11-83	20-10-82
Alice Packe	Pharsalia Plains	600	10-12-85	20-10-81
Edward Piner		600	23-11-83	21-12-83
John Price	Plains of Jericho	1200	20-8-85	20-10-80
Thomas Price	Howling Quarter	1000	5-12-85	17-8-82
Tho Peterson	Petersborough	500	17-12-85	20-10-81
Roger Patrick	Cornwall	1500	21-3-80	25-12-81
Rob Palmontary	Parington	400	3-12-84	25-1-82
Robert Parvis		600	20-9-83	17-8-82
Charles Pickering		200	10-1-87	
Thomas Pemberton		100	7-12-87	
John Richardson Sr.		158	6-10-83	21-10-80
John Richardson Sr.		130	11-10-83	21-10-80
John Richardson Sr.		1200	9-11-86	
Will Rodeney	Tanton	500	10-3-85	20-10-81
Daniel Rutty	Ruttington	400	12-12-85	21-12-81
John Robinson	Robertsbury	400	14-12-85	20-10-81
John Rawlins Sr.	Golden Minne	500	21-12-85	21-10-80
John Rawlins Jr.	Longford	600	15-12-85	21-10-80
John Roades		1000	23-1-84	21-12-81
John Richardson & Fra. Whitwell		1800	29-1-80	9-9-83
John Sharpe		427	10-11-83	21-1-82
Henry Stevenson	Skarborrough	558	21-12-83	20-10-81
Thomas Stratton	Sittingburne	500	9-11-84	20-10-81
William Spencer	Bridgetowne	1000	21-11-85	15-9-81
George Sheppard	Chasford	400	12-12-85	21-12-81
Tho Skidmore	Skidmore	400	20-12-85	21-7-80
Thomas Selby	Wells	1000	20-3-86	21-12-81
John Sharp	Sharpburn	300	20-12-85	17-8-82

5

Wm Sharnes	Sherwood's pchse	900	9-12-86	21-10-80
Wm Shore	Golden Thicket	400	10-5-86	25-9-81
Widdow Sample	The Vinyard	600	6-12-84	19-2-81
Frances Simon & Elizabeth Irons		300	10-11-86	
James Shakley		600	10-11-86	
James Shakley & John Richardson Jr.		1237	10-11-86	
William Tribet	Tripington	300	19-11-83	21-12-81
Jeffry Thomson	Westmoreland	300	24-4-84	
Jeffry Thomson	(old grant)	200	24-4-84	
John Vickory		400	13-11-83	21-10-81
Corn Verhoof &	Goosbery	600		
Peter Groenendik				
William Winsmore	Pipe Elm	778	11-8-83	
William Winsmore		100	10-12-86	
Thomas Williams	Leverpool	101	10-1-84	
Thomas Williams	Billingate	30	20-3-85	
Richard Williams	Richmore	300	2-12-85	21-1-82
Richard Williams		600	14-9-84	21-10-80
Alexander Williams	Bark	400	17-3-86	21-12-81
William Williams	Bloomsberry	300	29-12-83	15-1-81
Rinier Williams	Angell Ford	744		
Luke Watson Sr	Hunting Quarter	1500	4-12-85	21-12-81
Luke Watson Jr	Heyfield	500	5-12-85	15-6-82
Richard Walker	Leadernock	600	27-12-85	17-8-81
Thomas Walker		800	12-11-83	20-4-82
William Winsmore	Winsmores Dale	300	14-12-85	17-9-80
Harman Wilbank	Longfield	1000	22-12-85	15-1-81
Aminadab Wright	Lincolne	400	20-4-83	20-3-80
James Wells	Howells Lot	1000	25-11-82	21-12-81
Pattrick Word	Kingsdale	600	5-1-84	21-7-80
Wm & Tho Wilson	The Wm & Thomas	129	9-12-85	
Thomas Wilson	Derby Towne	1200	27-12-84	18-3-77
Richard Wilson	The Mount	400	17-10-85	12-7-80
Richard Wilson	The Vale of Fountain	300	17-10-85	21-1-81
Francis Whitwell		1000	30-3-80	26-1-84

Richard Whitehall 400 2-10-87 20-10-81

SUSSEX COUNTY RENT ROLL, 1681-1688

William Arundell	Arundell	300	2-2-85	13-10-76
John Avery	The Island	210	7-2-85	
John Avery	Golden Quarter	300	8-12-85	
John Avery	Cliftons Hall	216	26-12-87	
Daniel Andrew	Cedarton	600	9-1-86	10-8-81
Garret Barnes		300	18-11-81	12-4-84
John Bellamy	Pleasant	1000	30-3-84	1-9-84
Robert Bracy		300	19-1-85	
Henry Bowman	Bowmans farms	3000	23-1-85	
Hen Bowman	Golden Bower	800	16-1-86	
Tho Bostock	Sypres Hall	400	13-1-86	
John Barker	Crostowne	200	1-10-87	
Tho Bessant		500	14-10-87	14-1-81
Wm Bradford	Bradfords Hall	1200	1-1-85	
Charles Bright	Pensey	180	14-2-88	
Norton Claypoole		2000	10-4-82	8-6-85
John Cropper	Ladyes Delight	1000	19-2-84	6-12-81
Abraham Clement	Milbourne	100	13-1-85	
William Clark		800	6-1-86	
Francis Corwall	Greenfield	100	12-4-86	10-8-85
William Carter	Stretchers Hall	500	15-10-87	
David Coursey	Spooners Corner	300	16-10-87	
Stephanusvan Cortland	Bowmans Farm	1200	23-12-84	15-4-81
Andrew Depree	Fairfield	645	18-2-84	18-8-82
Alexander Draper	Little Bolton	1000	11-2-82	
Daniel Darby		600	13-7-86	15-1-82
John Dixon	Dixons Berry	400	8-2-86	
Mathias Everson		375	10-1-85	23-4-79
John Finch	Finches Hall	650	13-2-86	15-4-81
James Gray		1000	10-3-86	11-12-81

7

Yoakam Gulick	Waton	400	18-7-86	15-4-81
Thomas Hall	Harkles Plains	470	17-2-84	18-8-82
Charles Hall	Pleasant Farms	1000	17-1-86	20-4-82
John Hill	Branston	430	10-12-84	16-6-84
Rob Hart Junr	Harts Range	900	4-3-85	23-10-77
Rob Hart Junr	Marsh	30	4-3-85	15-9-81
John Haggister	Hassard	400	27-5-85	11-4-81
Arthur Johnson VanKirk		375	5-3-85	
Cornelius Johnson	Brownbury	400	6-1-86	
Cornelius Johnson		400	13-2-88	
Robert Johnson	Golam	700	20-2-88	
William Jerman	Newcoms burrow	400	13-5-85	4-10-76
William Jerman	Bourne	400	13-2-88	4-10-76
Arthur Julous	Gosberry	300	1-10-87	
John Kiphaven	Nonsuch	500	12-3-84	14-12-81
John Kiphaven	Kickout	700	17-9-87	
Wm Kenny		300	30-1-85	15-1-82
Jno Kerk		800	11-10-84	
Rowly vanKerk	The Berry	400	14-1-86	21-7-80
Daniell Lake	Pashalia	700	12-1-86	
Richard Lawes	Lawes Chance	300	20-2-85	19-1-81
Alexander Mouleston	Cades Delight	1000	13-3-84	
George Middleton	North Hartford	600	10-1-87	
Thomas Nixon		400	4-3-85	4-4-77
Baptist Newcomb	Ranglinton	400	4-2-87	
John Okey	Morlatto Hall	800	18-2-84	2-2-84
John Okey	White Horse	400	16-3-84	
Mathew Osborn	Woodberry	300	4-3-85	24-4-82
Richard Partty	Wheelers Hall	200	14-5-85	23-9-76
Abraham Potter		300	6-1-86	
Henry Peddington		400	8-1-86	
Henry Peddington		400	18-1-86	12-11-79
John Rye	Emmet Hall	800	28-3-87	12-7-84
Anthony Parsley	Blacksmiths Hall	300	17-10-87	
William Playner	Prices Haven	750	26-10-87	14-6-81

Name	Place			
John Roades & Rickson White	Whitehall	500	28-11-85	15-1-82
Henry Smith		600	5-3-84	
John Smith		300	6-1-86	15-1-82
John Sturges	Stratford	1000	1-2-85	8-4-77
Richard Shoulder	Shellaway	300	4-3-85	16-7-81
Wm Spencer Senr		500	6-3-85	
Wm Spencer Junr	Timberneck	600	10-1-86	15-9-81
Wm Simonds		400	4-1-86	11-2-82
John Savage		800	5-1-86	13-10-81
Henry Skidmore	Farmers Delight	800	11-1-86	20-4-82
Charles Spooner	Spooners Hall	300	14-2-86	11-1-82
John Street		400	2-4-86	8-1-81
Jeremy Scott	Pasture Poynt	46	19-2-88	
Thomas Tilton	Rich Farme	650	13-2-86	15-4-81
Robert Twilly	Twillington	400	4-7-86	
Katherin Taylor		500	16-4-82	8-6-85
John Vines	Barkin	500	12-3-84	
John Vines		550	6-1-86	
John Vines		675	2-7-86	
Cornelius Verhoof	Cornhill	1200	15-11-87	13-1-87
Cornelius Verhoof	Point Lookout	1000	15-11-87	2-2-82
Cornelius Verhoof	Pews Hill	290	16-11-87	3-8-75
Cronelius Verhoof	Peters Berry	500	10-11-87	2-2-75
Luke Watson		500		
Luke Watson Junr		300		
Luke Watson		600	5-1-84	1-4-84
Luke Watson Junr	Lebanon	600	16-1-84	1-3-85
Luke Watson	Watsons Marshes	2049	14-12-84	1-3-85
Jno & Saml Watson	Pickwick	600	14-12-84	1-3-85
Tho Welborne	The Cheat	775	13-3-84	
Francis Williams	Cornberry	400	9-2-85	30-5-82
Edward Williams	Road plantation	500	6-1-86	24-12-81
Rich Williams	Fountain	600	19-7-84	
Wm Willet	Little Stratford	600	1-10-87	

9

Nathaniel Walker		90	4-3-85	27-4-84
Stephan Whittman	Ditchers Hall	600	26-3-85	11-2-82
Arthur Woolgast	Choyse	400	13-5-85	26-12-86
Halmanus Woolbank		400	26-5-85	
George Yong	Longbeach	300	30-1-85	26-7-81

1693 TAX ASSESSMENT LIST
THREE LOWER COUNTIES ON DELAWARE
NEW CASTLE COUNTY

NAME	VALUE	RATE
John Forat	240	1 - -
Henry Williams	360	1 10 -
Margaret Sherry	-	- 6 6
Edward Lison	300	1 5 -
Engelbert Lott	72	- 6 -
John Bisk	100	- 8 4
Jacobus Alrichs	-	- 6 -
John Williams	500	2 1 8
Edward Lillington	240	1 - -
Richard Hallywell	600	2 10 -
George Lamb	100	- 8 4
Jeffery Martin	300	1 5 -
Matthias Vanderheyden	240	1 - -
Johannes deHaes	360	1 10 -
Roeloff deHaes	-	- 6 -
Abraham Inloes	100	- 8 4
Katherine Harms	100	- 8 4
John Donaldson	360	1 10 -
Peter Perdrio	120	- 10 -
Leonard Otterhaven	100	- 8 4
Thomas Langshaw	-	- 6 -
John Blanchard	300	1 5 -
George Hogg	150	- 12 6

10

Richard Griffin	-	- 6 -
George Cook	100	- 8 4
John White, est.	72	- 6 -
Paul Barns	-	- 6 -
Mary William	360	1 10 -
Johannes Sardyne	-	- 6 -
Peter Alrichs	600	2 10 -
Sigfridus Alrichs	-	- 6 -
Hermanus Alrichs	-	- 6 -
Joseph Clayton	-	- 6 -
Cornelius Kettle	-	- 6 -
Matthias deRingh	100	- 8 4
Zecheriah Vanderenline	120	- 10 -
John Abrams	-	- 6 -
Joseph Moor	-	- 6 -
John Reynolds	-	- 6 -
John Hales	-	- 6 -
Hybert Lawrence	100	- 8 4
Otto Michael	-	- 6 -
John Cann	480	2 - -
Silvester Garland	120	- 10 -
James Claypoole	150	- 12 -
Reynier Vanderenline	300	1 5 -
Henry Vanderburgh	100	- 8 4
Edward Blake	300	1 5 -
Elias Scott	-	- 6 -
James Read	120	- 10 -
Jacob Vangezell	100	- 8 4
John Watts	200	- 16 8
George Moor	-	- 6 -
Humphrey Best	-	- 6 -
William Crosee	-	- 6 -
Isaac Seloover	-	- 6 -
Roger Wotton	120	- 10 -
Nicholas Daniel Price	-	- 6 -

11

Name		
Ambrose Baker	200	- 16 8
Richard Reynolds	100	- 8 4
Gerhard Smith	100	- 8 4
John Dunn	100	- 8 4
John Holt	-	- 6 -
Edward Cole	-	- 6 -
Henry Blackman	-	- 6 -
James Baker	-	- 6 -
Edward Land	-	- 6 -
Roger Lewden	-	- 6 -
Adam Short	-	- 6 -
John Clark	-	- 6 -
Anthony Battenborough	-	- 6 -
Edward Harrison	-	- 6 -
Peter Godin	100	- 8 4
Simon Marcillatt	-	- 6 -
William Tornson	-	- 6 -
Cornelus Huggins	-	- 6 -
Peter Dean	-	- 6 -
Timothy Kelly	-	- 6 -
Adam Hay	100	- 8 4
Martha Martin	-	- 6 -
John Sybrant	-	- 6 -
Artman Hayn	100	- 8 4
John Jaquett, est.	100	- 8 4
Erick Erickson	-	- 6 -
Nicholas Lockier	200	- 16 8
Sybrant Johnson	100	- 8 4
Henry Evertson	-	- 6 -
Matthias Malson	100	- 8 4
Henry Lemen's est.	100	- 8 4
John Matson	-	- 6 -
Jacob Clawson	100	- 8 4
David Richardson	-	- 6 -
Peter Jacquett	100	- 8 4

Adrian Johnson	-	- 6 -
Urin Botesman	-	- 6 -
Olle Powlson	100	- 8 4
Luke Emly	-	- 6 -
Charles Rumsy	120	- 10 -
John Rumsy	-	- 6 -
Robert Dyer	-	- 6 -
John Pennington	-	- 6 -
John Garrison	150	- 12 6
Robt. Hutchinson	120	- 10 -
John Smith	-	- 6 -
John Gardner	-	- 6 -
John Garretson, Jr.	100	- 8 4
Francis Land	-	- 6 -
David Vaughan	-	- 6 -
Peter Moline	-	- 6 -
Niel Cook	-	- 6 -
Matthias de Vos	-	- 6 -
Thos. Matthews	-	- 6 -
Oliver Matthews	-	- 6 -
Geo. Harland	100	- 8 4
Thomas Child	-	- 6 -
John Grigg	-	- 6 -
Charles Springer	-	- 6 -
Erick Anderson	-	- 6 -
Robert Bryan	-	- 6 -
Timothy Mellany	-	- 6 -
John Hendrick	-	- 6 -
Thomas Metcalfe	-	- 6 -
Henry Jacobs	-	- 6 -
Erasmus Steedham	-	- 6 -
Widow Stalcup	240	1 - -
Christian Urinson	-	- 6 -
Lawrence Eustason	-	- 6 -
Thomas Pearson	-	- 6 -

James Davis	-	- 6 -
-?- Parker	-	- 6 -
Bryan Mackdonnell	-	- 6 -
Hugh Simons	-	- 6 -
George Read	-	- 6 -
Philomy Morphey	-	- 6 -
Widow Robinson	250	1 - 10
William Ball	-	- 6 -
Thomas Wollaston	100	- 8 4
John Brewster	100	- 8 4
John Granham	100	- 8 4
Edward Green	-	- 6 -
Anthony Woods	-	- 6 -
Henry Jacobs, son	-	- 6 -
Daniel at Richardsons	-	- 6 -
Thomas Bedford	-	- 6 -
Robert Courtny	-	- 6 -
John Ogle	100	- 8 4
Joseph Moor	-	- 6 -
John Reynolds	-	- 6 -
Jonas Asham	100	- 8 4
Walter Crapp	-	- 6 -
Thomas Ogle	100	- 8 4
John Ellis	-	- 6 -
Christopher White	-	- 6 -
Wm. Rakestraw's est.	60	- 9 -
John Champion	-	- 6 -
Wm. Brown	-	- 6 -
Olle Thomas	120	- 10 -
John Nomers	120	- 10 -
John Latham	-	- 6 -
Peter Poulson	-	- 6 -
Paul Garretson	-	- 6 -
Henry Garretson	-	- 6 -
Thomas Sawyer	-	- 6 -

John Cock	-	-	6	-
Samuell Underwood	-	-	6	-
Aron Johnson	100	-	8	4
Conrade Constantine	-	-	6	-
Peter Stalcup	100	-	8	4
Henry Urinson	-	-	6	-
John Hans	240	1	-	-
Widdow Peterson	100	-	8	4
John Richardson	240	1	-	-
Urin Anderson	-	-	6	-
Broer Sinex	240	1	-	-
James Anderson	-	-	6	-
Peter Mounson	-	-	6	-
William Guest	100	-	8	4
Joost Stoll	-	-	6	-
Robert Robinson	100	-	8	4
William Robison	-	-	6	-
Richard Mankin	120	-	10	-
William Dixon	-	-	6	-
Gisbert Walraven	120	-	10	-
Jonas Walraven	-	-	6	-
Lulif Steedham	100	-	8	4
John Vans	-	-	6	-
George Whiteside	-	-	6	-

Christiana Precinct

Lucas Steedham	100	-	8	4
Francis Smith	-	-	6	-
William Vanderveer	-	-	6	-
John Vanderveer	-	-	6	-
Jacob Vanderveer	100	-	8	4
Cornelius Empson	500	2	18	8
Paul Peterson	-	-	6	-
Hans Peterson	300	1	5	0
Jacob Clements	-	-	6	-

15

Peter Mons	-	- 6 -
John Toarson	100	- 8 4
Peter Peterson	120	- 10 -
Thomas Nixon	-	- 6 -
Morgan Diewett	100	- 8 4
John Grubb	200	- 16 8
Henry Reynolds	120	- 10 -
Olle Rawson	20	- 1 8
John Clowd	100	- 8 4
Jeremiah Clowd	-	- 6 -
John Buckly	100	- 8 4
Olliver Cope	100	- 8 4
John Prew	-	- 6 -
Timothy Atkins	-	- 6 -
William Lester	100	- 8 4

Between Brandywine and Naamans Creeks

Valentine Hollingsworth	100	- 8 4
Thomas Hollingsworth	-	- 6 -
George Robison	-	- 6 -
Thomas Jones	-	- 6 -
Henry Toarson	-	- 6 -
Laci Curvehorn	-	- 6 -
George Lester (moved)		
William Pool	100	- 8 4
Alexander Finloe (ran away)		
Richard Beacham	-	- 6 -
Thomas Each	-	- 6 -
George Cowlson	-	- 6 -
Edward Long	-	- 6 -
Joseph Cloud	-	- 6 -
Henry Hollingsworth	50	- 4 2
Peter Baynton	100	- 8 4

1693 TAX ASSESSMENT LIST - NEW CASTLE COUNTY

Red Lion Precinct

Hans Hanson	150	- 12 6
John Moll	240	1 - -
William Woodland	120	- 10 -
John Darby	100	- 8 4
Richard Hudden	-	- 6 -
Anthony Smith	-	- 6 -
Richard Crawford	-	- 6 -
Peter Oalson	-	- 6 -
Henry Oalson	-	- 6 -
Peter Broadberry	-	- 6 -

George Creek and Appoquinimink Precinct

John Heally	100	- 8 4
Peter King	-	- 6 -
Bartholomew King	-	- 6 -
Marinus De Witt	-	- 6 -
Henry Walraven	100	- 8 4
Henry Walraven, Jr.	-	- 6 -
Edward Gibbs	300	1 5 -
Edward Braning	-	- 6 -
Ellis Humphrey	240	1 - -
Robert Ashton	300	1 5 -
Abell Dodd	-	- 6 -
John Hales	-	- 6 -
Hybert Lawrence	100	- 8 4
Otto Michael	-	- 6 -
Saml. Brewerton	-	- 6 -
William Pattison	100	- 8 4
Thomas Rothwell	-	- 6 -
Sampson Atkins	100	- 8 4
George Williams	-	- 8 4
Thomas Coon	-	- 6 -
Matthias Erixon	-	- 6 -
Richard Hambly	100	- 8 4

Isaac Vickeridge	-	- 6 -
Adam Peterson	240	1 - -
William Scarfe	-	- 6 -
John Sandidge	-	- 6 -
William Burrows	100	- 8 4
James Hews	-	- 6 -
William Howe	-	- 6 -
John Howe	-	- 6 -
John Burford	-	- 6 -
John Wilson	120	- 10 -
James Williams	-	- 6 -
John Pearson	-	- 6 -
Rowlif Anderson	300	1 5 -
Widow Andree	100	- 8 4
John Sykes	-	- 6 -
John Bolton	-	- 6 -

Duck Creek Precinct

Joseph England	150	- 12 6
Morris Liston	150	- 12 6
Peter Byard	360	1 10 -
Thomas Graim	-	- 6 -
Francis Letts	100	- 8 4
Richard Laws	-	- 6 -
Joseph Alman	100	- 8 4
Daniel Mackarty	-	- 6 -
John Taylor	100	- 8 4
Christopher Bening	-	- 6 -
Francis Wetsworth	-	- 6 -
William Osbourn	120	- 10 -
John Ball	100	- 8 4
Lewis Owen	-	- 6 -
Robert Batty	-	- 6 -
John Mackarty	-	- 6 -
Percifull Westingdale	-	- 6 -

1693 TAX ASSESSMENT LIST - NEW CASTLE COUNTY

Laurence Parker	-	- 6 -
Isaac Wheeldon	200	- 16 8
John Washington	-	- 6 -
Turlus Stulerant	-	- 6 -
William Grant	120	- 10 -

Collections by Edward Lillington

James Miller	500	2 1 8
John Burgrave	-	- 6 -
John Bishmore	100	- 8 4
Basil Stone	-	- 6 -
Wm. Ball	100	- 8 4

Collections by Adam Peterson

Casparus Herman	300	1 5 -
Edward Lillington, New Castle and Christina Creek		93 1 -
John Grubb, Brandywine and Naaman's Creek		15 18 6
John Darby, Red Lion		4 12 10
Adam Peterson, George and Appoquinimink Creek		18 - 8
Joseph England, Duck Creek		11 3 -

Total collected		142 16 -

1693 TAX ASSESSMENT LIST
THREE LOWER COUNTIES ON DELAWARE
KENT COUNTY

NAME	VALUE			
Duck Creek Hundred				
Cpt. George Martin, est,	300			
Henry Morgan, est.	150			
Henry Payremaine	100			
Jethro Thompson	100			
Edward Lowde	100			
Robert Palmetary	100			
Richard Hambly	150			
John Albertson	100			
Charles Hillyard	100			
Joseph Growdon	400			
John Hillyard	230			
Richard Turner	100			
John Bradshaw	100			
Richard James	100			
William Greene	100			
William Sherrer	200			
Robert Draughton	100			
Francis Huggins	100			
William Willson	100			
	2730	10	19	2

Not otherwise rated--to pay 6/ per head

Walter Jones
Lancelot Jones
John Nacarroe
Jon. Mackdaniell
Francis Betton
John Craven

2 2   Total for hundred -13 1 2

Little Creek Hundred

Richard Willson	500
John Richardson	700
William Freeland	500
Parnell Richardson	200
Simon Hirons	300
Thomas Gennefells for Griffith Jones	200
Arthur Allstone	100
Thomas Sharp	200
Thomas Willson, Jr.	100
Vebanus Tompson	100
Edwd Starkey for Needham	100
Thomas Bowlstock	150
John Kelley	100
Christopher Standley	100
Total	3150

Rated at 6/ per head:
John Willson
Thomas Clifford
Timothy Carron
Robert Porter
George Sharp
Robert Palmetary
Dennis Tobisson
John Barnes
Richard Makins
Isaac Stone

	3 - -
	13 2 6
Total for Hundred	16 2 6

Dover Hundred

William Morton, est.	150
James Clayton	100

Gabriel Jones	150	
James Maxwell	150	
Thomas Willson, Sr. for Wm. Winsmore's est		200
John Chant	100	
Georg. Morgan	100	
John Smith	150	
Saml. Burbary	200	
Richard Basnet	200	
John Courtney	100	
John Burton	200	
Arthur Meston	100	
Cpt. John Brinckloe	500	
Danl. Jones, Sr.	550	
Wm. Dickerson	200	
3100		

Rated at 6/ per head:
Isaac Freeland
John Lane
George Clifford
Patrick Harwood
Abraham Jarret
Jasper Jessop
Andrew Miller
Jacob Smith
Wm. Winsmore
Abell Willson
Matthew Willson
Thomas Shaw
Thomas Everet
Alexander Chance
Thomas Waddle
Samuel Hill
John Clayton
Thomas Cambell

Wm. Tommas
Wm. Parry
John Rude
John Fostegue
Mark Everett
Timothy Durell

Total for Hundred

7 4 -   12 10 10
19 14 0

Murderkill Hundred
John Howell's est   100
Wm. Lawrence & Michael Walton   60
Thomas Bedwell   100
Daniel R-?-ity   200
Peter Loober   100
Robert Hudson   100
Owen Garvey   100
Thomas Rouse   250
Richard Bugbey   100
Thomas Heather   100
Robert Edmonds   150
Stephen Simons   100
Peter Groenendick   300
Thomas Skidmore, Jr.   100
John Townsend   100
William Darvall   300
John Barnes   200
William Rodeney   150
John Robinson   150
                                              3010

Rated at 6/ per head:
John Shepard
John Evans
Thomas Flowers

23

George Hart
Thomas Nichols
Robert Bedwell
Adam Fisher
James Stones
Matthew Green
Richard Walls
William Nickolls
Robert Nickolls
Edmd. Needham
John Clark
Cornelius Cullin
John Shearly
Robt. Sidbottom
Thomas Miller
Annanias Turner

5 14 -
12 10 10
18 4 -

Mispillion Hundred
John Walker's est.	200
John Curtis	750
William Manloe	380
Mark Manloe	300
George Manloe	300
Wm. Freeman	150
Hugh Luff	100
George Robinson	150
Thomas Williams	100
Michael Donaho for Samson Allin	100
Richard Willson for Robert Hall's est.	100
Thomas Skidmore	200
Reynier Williams	200
Richard Williams	200

Daniel Browne	200
John Mills	150
Richard Curtis	150
Richard Hogbin	150
Luke Manloe	150
Wm. Clark	200
	4530

Rated at 6/ per head:
John Maroney
Georg. Twilley
William Barker
Thomas Joyce at the widow Makitt's
Richard Murrough
Georg. Cullin
Edwd. Killingsworth

	2 2 -
	18 17 6
Total for Mispillion Hundred	20 19 6

Murderkill	18 4 10
Little Creek	16 2 6
Dover	19 14 10
Duck Creek	13 1 2
Total for Kent County	88 2 10

Taxes paid at:
Mispillion--Thomas Skidmore's or Wm. Freeman's landing
Murderkill--Thos. Heatherd's or John Barnes' landing
Dover--Gabriell Jones' or Richard Barsnet's landing
Little Creek--Parnell Richardson's or Urias Cannon's landing
Duck Creek--Fast Landing or John Hillyard's landing

Collectors:
Richard Jones--Little Creek and Duck Creek
Daniel Jones--Dover
Thomas Bedwell--Murderkill
Richard Hogbin--Mispillion

/s/ John Brinckloe
William Manloe
John Walker

1693 TAX ASSESSMENT
THREE LOWER COUNTIES ON DELAWARE
SUSSEX COUNTY

NAME	VALUE	RATE
William Clark	700	2 18 4
William Swetman	500	2 1 8
Comfort Scott and chn.	500	2 1 8
William Owen	500	2 1 8
John C-?-	500	2 1 8
Adam B-?-	500	2 1 8
Peter Lewis	500	2 1 8
Peter Raymon and R. Corbitt	300	1 5 0
Tho. Branscomb and chn.	300	1 5 0
Robt. Clifton and chn.	300	1 5 0
James Johnson	300	1 5 0
William Dyre and bros.	300	1 5 0
Henry Bowman	300	1 5 0
Tho. Groves and chn.	300	1 5 0
Henry Stretcher	250	1 0 10
Widow Wynne	250	1 0 10
Cornelius Wiltbank	250	1 0 10
Thomas Fisher	250	1 0 10
John Hill	250	1 0 10

John Stockly	200	0 16	8
Robert Burton	200	0 16	8
Alexander Mouliston	200	0 16	8
Samuell Preston	200	0 16	8
Josia West and chn.	200	0 16	8
Samuell Gray	200	0 16	8
Arthur Glass	200	0 16	8
Jacob Collick	200	0 16	8
William Piles	200	0 16	8
Jacob Waring	200	0 16	8
William Burton	200	0 16	8
John Barker	150	0 12	6
Hercules Sheperd	150	0 12	6
Morris Edwards	150	0 12	6
Albart Jacobs	150	0 12	6
Widow Baggwell	150	0 12	6
Jonathan Baley	150	0 12	6
Thomas Pemberton	150	0 12	6
Bryant Rowles	150	0 12	6
Barnes Garritt	150	0 12	6
Joseph Booth	150	0 12	6
John Richards	150	0 12	6
Art Johnson Vankirk	150	0 12	6
Thomas Tilton	150	0 12	6
Woodman Stockly	100	0 8	4
Peter Waples	100	0 8	4
Matthew Stephens	100	0 8	4
Thomas Jones and chn.	100	0 8	4
John Turbury	100	0 8	4
Robert Tomlinson	100	0 8	4
Robert Bracey, Sr.	100	0 8	4
Anthony Enlocs	100	0 8	4
William Simons	100	0 8	4
Richard Law	100	0 8	4
Thomas Besert	100	0 8	4

Joseph Allit	100	0 8 4	
Richard Harvey	100	0 8 4	
John Williams	100	0 8 4	
James Peterkin	100	0 8 4	
Mikel Chambers	100	0 8 4	
Nehemiah Field	100	0 8 4	
Adam Johnson	100	0 8 4	
Thomas Oldman	100	0 8 4	
John Miers	100	0 8 4	
Charles Wright	100	0 8 4	
Anthony Haverla	100	0 8 4	
Richard Cox	100	0 8 4	
Abraham Sotter	100	0 8 4	
Thomas Manloe	100	0 8 4	
Henry Spencer	100	0 8 4	
John Wattson	100	0 8 4	
William Emmatt	100	0 8 4	
Nathaniel Seks	100	0 8 4	

Assessed at 6/ per head

Charles Stockly	William Atkins	Edward Dembrick
Thomas West	Joseph Mayner	John Pettyjohn
Joseph Burkill	John How	Charles at Waples'
Richard Gill	Thomas Franklin	James Atkin
Aminidab Hanger	Francis Johnson	John Oakey, Sr.
Abra. Moleston	Francis Williams	John Pitts
John Bryer	Robert Barber	John Streate, Sr.
John Streate, Jr.	Richard Ward	Richard Drarey
Edward Williams	John Jones	John Graves
Samuel Graves	Jonathan Wynne	James Wilson
Timothy Dounjon	Ben Crosley	John Jennings
Thomas Cramer	Gabriel Jones	Henry Bowman, Jr.
Thomas Woods	John Usband	John Depree
Jacob Depree	Richard Shaw	James Heath
Thomas Midgely	Will Davids, shoemaker	Mikel Clifton

Edward Gold	Ralph -?-	John Farwell
Philip Russel	Collins Cudwithe	Edward Page
Tho. Page	Richard Star	John Pey
John Harmerson	Charles Haynes	Simon Parling
William Whit	Richard Holliway	John Maxfields
John Brown	Richard Painter, Jr.	Wights Howard
William Woolfe	Anthony Parsley	Charles Spooner
John Davids	John Richards	Tho. Moleston
Tho. Coverdel	John Fox	Richard Dobson
Thomas Kearle	Matthew Osborne	John Fisher
Richard Rennolds	John Donavan	Thomas Willson
Will. Goldsmith	James Brown	John Manloe and his son
John Draper	Nicholas Granger	William Thomas
William Millner	Tho. Shire, Jr.	James Carpenter
Joseph Hickman	Will Stapleton	Will David, planter
John Manhon	-?- Whetman	Cesar Burton
Tim. Burton's tennant	Will Morsley	Charles Johnson
Thomas Clifton, Carp.	Will Parker	Henry Hamar
Alexander Grant	Thomas Farran	Jenkins Smith
John Askue	Thomas Sikes	William Gurling

Thomas Davis, Sr.	100	0 8 4	
Samuell Watson	100	0 8 4	
John Crew	100	0 8 4	
Richard Painter, Sr.	60	0 5 0	
Widow Dawson's land	25	0 2 1	
Baptis Newcomb	200	0 16 8	
Thomas May	200	0 16 8	
Widow Draper's chn.	200	0 16 8	
Luke Watson, Sr.	200	0 16 8	
John Williams' heirs	200	0 16 8	
Luke Watson, Jr.	200	0 16 8	

Total for Sussex County 101 1 9

/s/ Wm. Clark
Tho. Pemberton
Samuel Preston
Samuel Gray
Robert Clifton

KENT COUNTY, DELAWARE, QUITRENTS, C. 1701-1713

(Page 1)
Mispellan Hundred alias Miskmelon
26th February 1705/6
William Freeman 250 (acres) granted by patent to William Freeman
now Jn. Brinckloe's, tract named Freeland
Hugh Luffe 200 a. Purchased a Warrt. from Tho. Pemberton laid out by order of
Wm. Clark. . .to Adam Luffe the certificate being at Philadia. by Jno. Gilbert for
a Pat. he requests that it may be granted by a list of Wm. Clark Survey's there is
mentioned 100 acres surv'd. 10.4.86 by Th. Pemberton at 1 d per acre by there
called Manloe's bounds, he holds not this but has lett it fall because it came on
other men's bounds. Ye certif. for this does not appear.
Henry Molleston for Jonath. Manloe, Point Lookout on Strunkill at the bottom
of Mispellan Hundred. 300 a. granted by Patnt. from Wm. -?- to Jno. Curtis
survd. 14.8.87 by a warrt. for 1200 a's. dat. 21.12.81/2 rent at Dover 1 bu./yr. Jno.
Curtis by deed dat 7.9.87 granted it to Geo. Manloe whose widow H. Mol. married, it belongs to his son Jonath. Manloe.
More joyning on ye back of ye former called Manlove's Green 100 a's. conveyed
by Tho. Pemberton by deed dat. 7.4.90 to George Manloe it was granted by Pat.
dat. 29 Mar 94 to Tho. Pemberton survd. 7.10.89 by virtue of a warrt. from Kent
C. for 1000 a's dat. 19 July 82. Rent 1 bushel at Lewes.
Ditto for himself (Henry Molleston) Gooseberry on Misp. branches 600 a. con-
veyed by Da. Powel of Philadia. by deed dat. 8 May 97 to Hen. Mollestine
150 (acres) granted by pat. from Wm. M. (Markham) and J. Goods. dated
11.3.87 to Danl. James warrt. from Kent Court 21.10.80 survd. 20.12.85 rent at
Dover 1 bu. per 100 (acres).
Robt. Betts 150 (acres) sold him by Hen. Molleston about 3 years ago.
(Page 2)

Danl. Brown 300 a. survd 21.12.84 by a warrt. from ye court dat 15.7.87 as Will. Clark's certificate to Danl. Browne but was never patented the sd. Danl. bequeathed 100 acres of this to Mary now wife of Jno. Reynolds ye other his son Danl. holds desires a patent orders a resurvey.

Jno. Betts widow 530 (acres) part of 1000 acres granted by pat from H.C. and R.T. to Jno. Betts warrt. 21.10.80 rent at Dover 1 bushl. of wheat per c. (100 acres) of ye remaindr. Geo. Robinson holds 300 a's. and Jno. Hall 170 a's. Adjoining marsh 300 a. granted by pat. from W.M., R.T. and H.C. dat 14.5.94 to Jno. Betts warrt. from ye. commrs. 23.10.93 survd 16 Febry 93/4. Rent 1 bushl per c. (100 acres).

More 1000 a. laid out in ye forest about ye head of Murderkill from ye commrs. to Jno. Betts survd. by Willm. Morton they say it was by a warrt. at first of Jno. Brinckloe's, Saml. Burbery and Jno. Ridny carried ye chain the propr. promised a pat. but it must be resurvd.

Saml. Burbery produces also a warrt. for 1000 a's. from Tho. Holme dat 3.10.93 to Capt. Jno. Rodeney, Esq., & 200 a's. of marsh by virtue of a warrt. (is sd.) from ye Commrs. of Propty. This to be enquired into at Philda. & renewed. Ye warrt. is assign'd by Will Rod. attorney to Jno. Rod.'s widow & admx.

(Page 7)

Murderkill Hundred

26 Febry. 1705/6

Wm. Freeman 413 now 546 by res., survd. by Corn. Verhoof 13.9.79 by wart. from Whorekill Court dat. 10.7.79 to Peter Groundike for 413 acres taken by execution from Kent Court at a court held 8.10.96 at ye suit of Hen. Selyns & Mary his Wife exr. of Corn. Steenwick for a debt due to Steenwick in sd. Hen. & M. Sel. by deed dat. 4 June 98 conveyed it to Jacob Mauris & Johannes Provoost & Jno. vanGoden ye last being deceased the two first by deed dat. 4.8.1700 granted it to Wm. Freeman for 300 lbs. ye plantation free from all incumbrances with arrearage of quitrent his son W. Freeman holds it.

Adam Fisher 100 a. part of ye above Tract granted by Wm. Freeman Senr. with his daughter to Ad: Fisher about 4 yrs. ago.

Danl Rutty 280 (acres) Part of 800 a's. granted by pat. from ye propr. dat. 26.1.84 to Robt. Bedwell war from Kent Court 19.9.80 survd. 20.10.80 Rent at Cranbrook 1 bush. per c. (100 acres) Robt. Bedwell by indorsemt. dat. 16.4.85 assigned this to Hen Johnson & Danl. Rutty. H. Johnson conveyed his to Danl. Rutty who sold to Rd. Mitchel 400 now Fra. Richardson's 100 a's. to Wm. Trippet & 20 a's. to Mich. Loper.

31

<u>Fra. Richardson</u> 400 (acres) conveyed out of ye above 15.4.86 nothing paid.
(Page 8)
<u>Wm. Trippet</u> 100 (acres) purchased of the above 800 a's. 11 mo. 86.
Ditto called Trippington in ye. forrest, 300 (acres) granted by pat. from W.M. &
J.G. dat. 13.12.87 to Wm. Trippett war. from Kent Court 21.12.87 survd. 11.5.86
to W.T. Rent 1 bu. of wheat per c. (100 acres) at ye town of Dover.
<u>Michael son of Peter Loper</u> 20 (acres) part of Danl. Rutty's Tract purchased
about '86.
200 a's. granted by pat. from ye propr. dat. 26 1 mo. 84 to Jno. Courtney warrt.
from Kent Court 16.1.81 & sund. 12 mo. following to Henry Johnson and Danl.
Rutty who assigned their Right to Courtny. Rent at Cranbrood 1 bushl. of wheat
per c. (100 acres). . .This being sold to Courtney by Hen: Johnson & Danl. Rutty
he could not pay them D. Rutty informs that he took out ye par. therefore Henry
Johnson with his Wife & D. Rutty sold 221 acres being this 20 & 200 a's. by deed
dat. 15.7.84.
<u>Joseph Skidmore</u> 92 a's part of a tract formerly called Gibbon's Point now Dover
farm confirmed to W. Rodeny for 840 acres from the Prop. dat 8 mo. 1701.
<u>Michael O'Donohoe</u> 275 a's. part of 1100 acres granted by warrt. of St. Jones
Court dat. Feb. 21 81/2 survd. 7 of Mar. 81/2 by Ephr. Herman as per certif. in ye
servie's office transferred by pt. & recital to Tho. Bedwell, Hen. B. & Robt.
Bedw., Jr. & Ad. Fisher to whom it was laid out. Robt. Bedwell sold 275 a's of
this to Saml. Burbery who sold to Wm. Morton who by deed dat. 10.9.97 sold to
to M Odon: who has since sold 100 of ye 275 a's. to Wm. Rodeny. Of the rest
(no information given)
<u>Tho. Bedwell</u> 1050 a's. Folly Neck, 375, part of 1050 acres called Folly Neck wh.
was at first laid out for 800 a's. to Robt. Bedwell granted by pat. from Sr. Edmd.
Andros dat 20 6 mo. 1697--Resurvd. by warrt. on the 10th of ye 11th mo. 85 and
confirmed by patent for 1050 acres to Robt. Bedwell by W.M., R.T., & J.G. dat.
6 Mar. 90/91. Rent at Lewes.
More purchased of his brother Robert, 50 (acres) pt. of the same purchased lately but paid 4 rents by Robt. Bedwell in his tract of 175 a's. to 4 1 mo. 1707.
More of the above. 400 (acres) granted by a patent to Jno. Newell. Jno. Newell
sold it to Rd. Mitchel who sold to Danl. Jones who sold to Jno. Curtis whose
son Caleb sold it Robt. Bedwl. together with 150 acres more wch. D. J. at ye
same time sold with the above 400 a's. in one deed to Jno. Curtis & so to Robt.
Bedwell conveyed this to Robt. Webb in exch. for 200 acres.

More 250 called the Mill land. Part of 400 acres called Shoemaker's hall granted by Pat. to H. Webb.

The other 200 of this is held by John and Josh. Clayton who live in Little Cr. Hun.

Robt. Bedwell 125 a's. part of Holly Neck above granted to his father and namesake.

Henry Bedwell's heirs now Joshua Clayton 175 (acres) part of the Holly Neck above granted to his father Robt. Joshua Clayton owes on the Ball. of his Bond for this & John Robison's land.

Jno. and Joshua Clayton each 100 a's. Part of Shoemaker's Hall ye other moiety of ye 100 a's. He holds more that is lately purchased of Ja: Coutts' heirs Jno. Everet's land formerly and taken in execution, 138 a's.

(Page 10)

Robt. Hudson 800 a's. granted by warrt. from the Court 21 Feb. 81 was survd. 27.9.83 by Wm. Clarke certificate for -?- of return patented but was not produced.

Jacob Emerson 100 (acres) pt. of 300 acres granted by pat. to Robt. Edmonds. Robt. Edmonds by deed dat. convey'd to Jac. Emerson but he has since viz about 90 (1690) sold 50 a's. to Joseph Hilliard whose children have it.

Doct. John Boyer 100 a. Part of 2450 a's. of land in two tracts one of 1050 a's. granted by pat. from ye Propr. dat. 12.4.84 to Benoni Bishop wart. from Kent Court. Survd. 29.1.81 rent at ye pt. of Cranbrook 1 bush. per c. (100 acres) called Bishop's Choice and 1400 a's. called -?- Column survd. 21.4.85 by warrt.

The pat.	2450
Benoni Bishop sold to Rd. Wall	
about 86	500
to S. Mott abt. 86	200
the eldest daughter wife of Owen	
Garvie & her husbd. made over to	
Fra: Renolds ab.	200
to Jno. Townsend about 94	200
	1100

Ben. Bishop left 2 daughters ye. eldest married to Ow. Garvie who convey'd during her life but she dying w/out issue ye whole came to ye younger daughter Margt. who married Jno. Bowman who with his wife conveyed 100 a's more or less to Owen Garvie who sold this to Doctr. Boyer. Margt. Bowman ye ygr. daughter dying without issue all ye land unsold viz. 1250 a's. is escheated but (Page 11) Jno. Bowman and his wife sold 600 acres part of this deed to Robt.

Hudson but he dying before the conveyance he cannot make the bill to him. John Townsend desiring to purchase the rem. of B. Bishop's land for his children desires to know the terms.

Thomas Wells 100 (acres) part of 400 acres granted by pat. from the Propr. dat. 26.1.84 to David Morgan warrt from Kent Court survd. 2.10.80 Rent at Dover 1 bushl. per c. (100 acres). Morgan sold to Jno. Sheppard 100 a's. who sold to Jno. Nichols who sold to Geo: Hart who sold to Th: Wells 10.7.1700.

John Townsend 100 (acres) part of 200 acres purchased of Bishop ye other 100 resold to Garret Sipple.

Garret Sipple 100 (acres) the sd. moiety of 200 acres.

Rd. Walls 500 (acres) part of B. Bishop's land.

Thomas Skidmore 100 a. part of about 100 acres laid out to Nicholas Bartlet 16.12.85 by warrt. dat. 21.1.82.

Reb. and Esther Millar 100 a's. part of ye same all the rent due Wm. Gupton gave bond for ye arrears but is run away.

John Smith 200 a. purchased of Saml. Burberry about 1696 part of the same tract with the above of Nich. Bartlet, sold 100, holds now 100.

Edwd. Burroughs 100 (acres) the moiety of the 200 acres less the above sold by Jno. Smith.

(Page 12)

Fred: Philips 600 a. the remaindr. of the foregoing tract of Nich. Bartlet's 1000 a.

Elizab: Turner now Richd. Swan her husb 100 (acres) pt. of Holly Neck sold by Tho: Bedwell, 8 Febry 91., then 150 acres of wch. 50 are sold to Jno. Barnes about 13 years ago.

Richd. Jackson 130 (acres) part of Holly Neck entred pa. 9 purchased by him of Jno. Dubois by Decbr. 13.7.97 who purchd. the same of Mary Clayton by deed dat. 10.9.97 (some mistake in these dates but both deeds were made over in that 9 court).

Benjamin Dabbs 50 a. purchased by David Gogin of Danl. and Elen. Rutty by deed dat. 24 Apr. 1700 is pt. of Holly Neck entred pa. 9 conveyed by Gogin to B. Dabbs by a late deed dat. (date not given). More in Dover Hund. 570 a. entred in Dover Hund. pa. 15.

David Morgan 200 a. one moiety of 400 a's. granted to himself by the propr. pat. dat. 26.7.84 entred fully in Tho. Wells pa. 11.

The land is now held by   W. Annand 1/3 66 2/3 acres
                           Jno. Morgan 1/3 66 2/3 acres

Matth. Morgan 1/3 66 2/3 acres.

<u>George Hart</u> 100 a. part of the above mentioned 400 a's being ye left hund. purchased of Phebe exx. of David Morgan by deed dat. 12.10.93. More of Burton's Delight, 50 (acres). More of ye Long reach, 100 (acres), total 250 acres.
<u>Jno. Flowers' estate</u> entred in Dover where it lies p. 15.
<u>Timothy Thorrold</u> 50 a. 1/7th pt. of 350 a's bought of Tho: Bedwell by Ezekiel Needham who by Deed dat. 10 Aug. convey'd it to T. Thorrd.
(Page 13)
<u>Ezekiel Needham</u> now Edmd. Needham, 300 (acres) purchased of Tho: Bedwell he to clear all rents.
<u>Willm. Brinkloe</u> 391 a. part of a tract called Denbigh entred to Wm. Rodeny pa. 18.
(Page 15)
Dover or St. Jones Hundred, 27th
<u>Daniel Smith</u> admr. to Griff. Jones 145 a. purchased by Griff. Jones of Simon Hirons about 1692 who purchased of Wm. Berry and is pt. of a tract of (not given) acres called the New Design granted by (not given)
more, 50 a. purchased by Gr. Jones of Sam. Burberry by ded dat. 8.10.96 pt of ye same tract with the above purchased by S. Burberry of Wm. Morton by deed dat. 2 Mar 95.
<u>Jno. Flower's estate in Murderkill Hundred</u> Purchased by him of Wm. Lawrence & Nichs. Walton of Philadia. by deed dat. 11 Apr. 1701 being part of a tract formerly belonging to Danl. Toaes of Maryld. this they say is now taken by R. French for debt of J. Flower his relict is married to Danl. Goodin.
<u>George Morgan</u> 50 a. should be but 40 a. purchased of Jno Everet by deed dat. 20.7.88 who purchased of Jno. Richardson by deed dat. 15.2.84 being pt. of a tract of his called Northampton containing 240 a's. granted by pat. from ye propr. entred over ye leaf.
Item 60 (acres) purchased of Rd. Glover by deed dat. 27.3.90 said in ye deed to be laid out ye 25th of Mar. 1690. Robt. French has the pat. it was granted to Jno. Glover by warrt. from St. Jones survd 24.9.80.
Item 100 (acres) purchased of Jno. Chart by deed dat. 8th of Mar. 1692 is part of the tract next above mentioned called Cockhill.
<u>Benjamin Dabbs</u> 570 a. part of 670 acres called Concord granted -?- & recitall in Hiron's deed by a warrt. from Kent Court dat. 21.1.82 mo. for 500 a. survd. to Francis, Simon and Elizabeth Hirons & confirmed by pat. to them dat. 25 Febry. 1691/2 rent at Dover. This 570 Acres was convey'd by deed from Simon and

Francis Hirons dat. 2 Febry 92/3. It seem laid out 9 mo. 86 by W. C.-list in -?- that there is a tract to S. Hirons for 610 a. wart. 20.4.82.

(Page 16)

James Clayton's estate 100 a. convey'd by Jno. Burton to James Clayton by deed dat. 8th 9 mo. 87 being part of the land Jno. Burton then lived on.

Jno. Burton called Burton's Delight 600 (acres) including the above together with 150 a's of James FitzGerrard 50 of Henry Stevens' 50 of George Hart 70 of Capt. Rodeny ye remaindr. should be but 180 sold to Robt. French Burton has recvd. the rents for it because he was patentee.

Capt. John Brinckloe 180 a's. purchased of Robt. French

John Evans 100 pt. of 240 a's. granted by pat. from the propr. dat 12.4.84 to Jno. Richardson warrt. 21.7.80 for a greater tract but survd. only 240 a. 27.9.80 rent at Dover 1 bushl. per c. (100 acres).

Jno. Nicholson 100 (acres) pt. of ye foregoing purchased of Wm. Morton who purchased of Jno. Everet, who purchased of Jno. Richardson the other 40 a's. entred to Geo. Morgan

Willm. Winsmore Great Pipe Elm, 428 a. part of a tract of 778 acres called Great Pipe Elm granted by pat. from J. Clayp. & R. T. dat. 29.11.84 to Wm. Winsmore wart. from ye propr. 1.6.83 returnd. 13.3.83. Rent at Dover 1 bush. per c. Wm. Winsm. gave to Abel Wilson & Matthew & Reb. Wilson each 100 a's & his son Wm. since sold 50 a's. to Tho Wilson & holds the remaindr.
There was due to clear 478 a's. of Wm. Winsmore's and 263 a's. of his sister Mary's (quitrents due follow).

(Page 17)

Matthew Wilson's children 300 a's part of Great Pipe Elm given away by Wm. Winsmore about 1685 or 1686.

John Burton for his son Jasper Jessup 100 (acres) the other 100 acres given away by Wm. Winsmore being Reb: Wilson's share.

Elizab: Glover 263 a's. the title not made out but belonged to Wm. Winsmore & he gave it to his daughter Mary mother to the child Elizab: Glover.

Capt. John Brinkloe Poplar Ridge 400 (acres) made up of one tract of 260 acres called Poplar Ridge Granted by Pat. dat. 14 Aug. 1678 from Sr. E. Andros to Jno. Briggs who sold to Jno. Brinkloe.

& 258 acres granted by Pat. from W.M. R.T. & J.G. dat. 7 Jun 93 to John Brinkloe warrt. from Kent Court 21 Janry. 1681 survd. 12 Mar. 1691 rent at Dover 1 Bushl. per c. These two make 518 acres of wch. he sold Arhtr. Meston 103 acres.

Ditto. 300 a. One Moiety of 600 acres call'd Hillyards Adventure granted by pat from the propr. dat 1.1.84 to Simon Irons warrt. from Sussex Court blank survd. 26.9.79 to Jno. Hillyard who assign'd over his Right sold by them to T. Engld. who sold to Capt. Brinkloe young Simon Hirons holds ye remaindr.

Arthur Meston 103 Purchased of Jno Brinckloe being pt. of ye above 518 acres. (Page 18)

Richd. Levick 600 a. laid out in 2 tracts the one called Bridgeworth (?) by Rd. Noble 280 acres survd 30.9.1680 ye other in a tract of 320 survd. by Josh: Barkstead 9.6.1683 as per his certificate by warrt. from Kent Court 17.9.80 this is called Edenton both to Richd. Levick whose Son enjoys it these were confirmed by pat. they affirm but twas burnt with their house.

Desires a patent there are draughts in ye Secries office. Stephen Paradee now holds it (the 320 a. tract). More 200 a. entred in Little Cr: Hund. p. 24.

Solomon Miller 200 a. Part of 400 acres called Aberdeen granted by pat. from ye Propr. dat. 26.1.84 to Tho: Clifford warrt. survd. 11.10.80 Rent at Dover 1 bushl. per C. of the other 200 R. French holds 100 & Maurice Smith ye other T. Clifford sold this to Jno. Smith who sold to Maur. Smith their father.

Capt. Wm. Rodeny 850 a's. Byfield granted by Patent from W.M. & J.G. dat 7.7.88 to Danl. Jones warrt. 26.11.80 survey 5.12.86 rent at Dover 1 bushl per c. held of Frith Manor W.R. married D. Jones' daughter & heiress.

Denbigh 400 a part of a tract of 791 acres call'd Denbigh granted by pat. from ye comrs. W.M. & J.G. dat. 15.3.89 for Danl. Jones warrt from St. Jones court 2.10.1680 Rent at Dover 1 bushl. per c. held of Frith the other 391 acres are held by Wm. Brinkloe.

Burtons 70 a. a parcel of land purchased by Danl. Jones of Jno. Burton by deed dat: 12 Mar 1681 no quantity mentioned in ye deed but by ye survey is 70 acres & is part of Burton's old patent being recited in his deed in 81.

Pt. of London tract called Tiverton in Little Ck. Hund. 400 a's. granted in a tract of land of 1300 acres by pat. from ye propr. (Page 19) dat. 9.8.1701 granted by pat. from Sr. E. Andros to Jno. Stevens who convey'd ye said 1300 acres to Wm. Morton & Wm. Rodeny to whom joyntly the sd. new patt. is granted Wm. Morton & Wm. Rodeny by deeds of partition divided this into equal parts & W. Morton by deed dated 11.7.11 -?- released to W. Rodeny 650 acres his moiety under certain bounds of wch 650 a's. Steph. Perdue holds 70 acres Jno. Clayton 180 Wm.Morton holds of ye other moiety 530 Steph Perdue 50 & Saml. Berry 70 a's. Rent is from ye first survey.

37

Dover Farms 748 a. part of a tract called Dover Farms cont. in ye whold 840 a's granted by the propr. to Wm. Rodeney dat. 17.8.1701 survd. by vertue of a warrt. from St. Jones court on ye 21 Mar. 1684 rent after ye rate of one bushl from ye date of survey ye other 92 acres are held by Jos. Skidmore entred pa. 8 this as ye above no place of pay.

New part Pilton 598 granted by pat. from ye Kent Commrs. dat 1 Febry 1703 warr. by ye propr. ord. & special grant to Capt. Rodeney dat. 26.9.1701 survd. (no date given) Rent 6 Bushls. of wheat at Dover River from ye 1 of Mar. 1703.

Wedmore 344 taken in execution at ye suit of Tho: Atthow agst. ye estate of Wm. Darval being pt. of 500 acres Wm. Rodeney admr. on Atthows estate to pay debts convey'd it to Jonas Greenwood of whom Wm. Rodeny purchased it again It was at first laid out to Wm. Rodeny as he affirms & purchased of him by Wm. Darvall.. There appears a tract in W. Clark 1 list of 500 a's. survd. 10.2.85. Warrt. 20.10.81.

Of Richardson's 200 a. part of 600 acres granted by Pat. from Sr. Edm. Andros dat. 25 Mar. 76 to Wm. Stevens Rent yearly to his Royal Highness use 6 bushels of wheat. Stevens sold this to Jno. Richardson who sold to W.R.

Of Slaughter's 100 purchased of Jno. Slaughter by deed dat. 10 Aug. 1703 who purchased of Mich. Donohoe 11 Apr. 1703 pt. of Thos. Bedwell's Long Reach entred pa. 8.

(Page 20)

Wm. Rodeny Dr.

for Byfield	850 a.
for Denbigh	400 a.
for Burtons	70 a.
for Tiverton	400 a.
for Dover faurms	748 a.
for Pilton	598 a.
for Wedmore	344 a.
for Slaughters	100 a.
for Richardsons	200 a.
	3710 a.

Thos. Mahon 175 part of a tract of about 1000 acres as at first laid out call'd Berry's Range but holds not 800 a's. they say granted by pat. to Wm. Berry.

James & Robt. Maxwell 75 part of the same these are his wife's children by her former husband James Maxwell.

<u>Thomas England</u> on Tidbury Branch was called Concord, 1200 acres warrt.
Court of Kent 17.8.82 survd. 13.10.83 patent from J.C. & R.T.dat. 15.3.86 to
Robt. Betts & Jno. King recorded Pat. Book A fol. 149 sold by them to Jno.
Brinkloe who sold it 16.1.1685 to Danl Toaes who sold to Tho. England.
Flowers' Lott 1040 a. granted by ord. of Court to Jas. Wells survd. 25.1.1683 sold
to Jno. Howel who called it from ye prop. Howels' Lott granted to Danl. Toaes
of whose estate T. Engl. recovered it 1704.
Great Geneva 600 acres taken up in the year 1681 by some means granted to
Danl. Toaes of whom the sd. T. Engld. recovered it with ye former.
Half of ye Improvement on Duck Creek, 500 (acres) taken up.
(Page 21)
Little Creek Hundred, 28th 12 mo. 1705
<u>Tho. Sharp</u> 324 (acres) granted by pat. from ye Kent Commr.
Rem. 150 (acres) purchased by T. Sh: of Jno Walker, Taylor lately who bought of
Jno. Hilliard.
<u>Jno. Richardson's widow</u>, Willingbrook their homestead 1200 (acres) granted by
pat. from ye propr. dat. 7.9.83 to Jno. Richardson warrt. 11.8.80 survd 22.9.80
Rent at Cranbrook on ye 10th of March being ye vernal equinox 12 bushls.
winter wheat.
Swinford in Duck Creek Hundred 800 a. granted by Pat. from ye Propr. dat. 26 1
mo. 1684 to Michael Sinkis warrt. from Kent Court -?- survd 9.2.82 to be held of
Freith Mannr. rent on bushel of wheat per. c. Jno. Richardson took this afd. by
execution of debt.
The Range at ye head of Dover Creek 1000 a. granted by Pat. from W.M. & J.
Good. dat 30.5.88 to Simon Irons warrt from Kent Court 20.4.82 survd. 12.9.86 to
be held of Freith Manr. Rent at Dover 1 bushl of wheat per. c. Purchased of
Wm. Berry by Jno. Richardson by deed dat. 1.12.1689 purch. by Berry. They say
of Irons by Exchange.
<u>Benjamin Brady</u> Chippin Norton 800 (acres) granted by pat. from ye Propr. dat
9.4.83 to Simon Iron warrt. from Whorekill Clark survd. 21 10 mo.nexd held of
Freith rent at Cranbrook on ye 10th of Mar. 8 bushls. winter wheat purchased by
Jno. Richardson of Simon Irons. J. R. gave it to his grandson B. Brady.
(Page 22)
<u>Lodowick Hall</u> The Content (Widow Wilson's now Vincent Emerson son in
law) 410 acres granted by pat.from ye propr. dat 26.11.84 to Evan Davies warrt.
19.9.80 survd. 5 11th mo foll rent at Dover 1 bush. per c. Ev. Davies sold this to

Ev. Jones who sold to Hilliard who sold to Wm. Jacocks who by dat. 6.8.94 sold it to Robt. Hall father of ye -?- orphan.

His brother Jno. Hall in Mispell. Hund. 170 (acres) purchased of Jno. Foster by deed dat. 5.7.90 by Rob. Hall being part of Jno. Betts 1000 a's. entred pa. 2. On Muddy Branch Wheel of Fortune 300 a's. Richd. Wilson by his will gave Lod: Hall above mentioned 300 acres call'd the Wheel of Fortune but not to his heirs & assigns for wch. they doubt first Rd. Wilson's title & again think it scarce worth notice ye words heirs & assigns being left out in ye will.

In Musmellon 100 a's left also by Jno. McKeterick Eliz. Wilson now Emerson's father to her son Jno. Hall to 100 a's of land but a title was never made.

Jno. Clifford 50 a. purchased by Tho: Clifford of Jno. Richardson Junr. being pt of a tract called Simson Choice 400 acres.

Item 50 (acres) part of the same tract sold by Jno. Richardson Junr. by deed dat. 1.7.91 to Tho. Carron who devised it to this boy Jno. Clifford.

Arthur Meston 400 (acres) part of 800 a's. granted by pat. from the propr. dat (none given) to Arthr. Alston wch. he alienated 400 acres to Tho. Bostock to whose orphan grandchild Mary FitzGerrard it belongs.

(Page 23)

Patrick Wood, J. Linfall, 600 (acres) taken up by Pat: Wood they say 25 or 26 years ago but neither warrt. not pat. produced. Resurvd. by Jones Greenwood in ordr. to patent seated 28 years agoe Ev. Jones, affirms, Returned & contains 757 (acres), of this sold 50 a's now held by Jno. Foster.

John Kelly 400 (acres) Galloway Joyning on the former & taken up a title after but is in the same circumfrances with the other was resurvd. & contains 440 acres seated above 20 years they declare.

Robt. Porter 50 a. part of Simson's Choice 150 acres sold by Jno. Richardson Junr. to Robt. Porter Sen. & Jun. & Law. Porter dat. 8.7.90 pt. of 400 acres taken up by Simson who sold it to Jno. Richardson Senr. who gave it to his son of this 50 acres were sold to James Potter about 1702.

Jno. Foster 170 a's. Purchased of Mary Thomson Excx. of Urba: Tomson by deed dat. 10 Febr. 1700 who bought ye 70 acres of Pat. Wood by deed dat. 7.7.96 and ye other 100 acres of Matth: Mason (ye whole 800 acres) who purchased of Robt. Smith Esq. of Chester Com. Maryl. who purchased 800 a. the whole tract of Jno. Hillyard Junr. whose father Jno. Hillyard took it up then as the patent.

Item 100 more part of ye sd. tract of 800 a's. Allum's Cabin purchased of James Tobias by deed dat. 13 Mar 1700 who bought of Matth: Mason above mentioned.

This holds out but 600 they say Jno. French holds 300 & 100 to Arnd. Henrikson & 100 to Saml. Tho. Sahawn both at York.

Item 55 (acres) purchased of Griff Jones of Philadia. by deed dat. 6.8.98 to Jno. Foster being pt. of a tract of 175 called Shrewsberry entred in Tho. Gonsales.

Item 40 (acres) purchased of Simson's Choice sold by Jno. Richdsn. Junr. to Jno. Cheate by deed dat. 7.7.91 whose heir Jno. Foster holds it.

Total Jno. Foster 365 acres.

(Page 24)

Thomas Gonsalez, a Spand., 120 a's. part of 175 acres called Shrewsbury granted by pat. from ye Propr. dat 30.1.84 to Evan Davies warrt. 21.4.81 survd. 20.11.79/80 so says ye t. Rent at Dover 1 bushl. winter wheat for every c. Sold to Ja: Wells whose widow 17.12.85 conv'd it to Griff Jones being taken by some means in execution & sold by J. Jo. by deed 6.8.98.

Rd. Levick 300 (acres) granted by deed from J. Richardson by deed dat. 14 June 98 being pt. of 600 a's. of land granted to Wm. Stevens entred W. Rodeny pa. 19.

Jno. Richardson 200 (acres) part of ye same tract being ye remaindr. vid. ye entry to W. Rodeny in ye 200 acres call'd Richardson's.

Wm. Morton's excrs. Jno. French 300 part of Allom's Cabin entred to Jno. Foster vid. pa. 23 in Jno. Foster's 2d hund.

Timothy Hanson (no acreage or description given)

(Page 27)

Duck Creek Hundred 1 March 1705/6

Evan Jones 290 (acres) part of 410 acres confirmed to Evan Jones from the commr. of Property dat. 2.2.1705 laid out for 300 a's. by vertue of a warrt. from Kent Court dat. 24.7.81 for 400 a's. and so much being found on the resurvey ye whole was allowed to him paying the rents from the beginning for ye whole rent from ye first execution of the sd. warrt. at Jones 1 bushl. of wheat per c. of this tract John Necarrow holds 120 of ye remaindr. all this was Jno. Hillyards once -?- Ev. Jones took it up.

John Necarrow 120 the remaindr. of ye above purchased of Saml. Bourdat whose brother Peter Bourdet took this of Hillyard for a debt. deed from 23 May 1703.

The rect. here entred for 2240 a's. is made up of

   300 acres entred above

600 acres of Whitehall held by Jo: Greenwood 225 & 375 by R.   Wilson's heirs

800 acres of Allom Cabin held by Jno. Foster entred pa 23 & 24 this cannot belong to it.

300 acres of Charles Hillyard. Mother plantation.

426 acres called ye. Exchange.

2426 is 186 acres above ye quantity to be deducted out of this if ye rect. must be allowed but is villanous, Allom Cabin may be thrown out.

Charles Hillyard 300 a. granted by pat for 200 a's from ye propr. dat 1.1.84 to Jno. Hilliard warrt. blank survd. 9.11.79 rent at Cranbrook 1bushl per c. More charged pa. 29 426 (acres). & 100 a's more granted by pat. from W.M. & J.G. dat. 10.8.87 to Oliver Hillyard his elder brother upon whose decease it fell to Charles & makes 300 a's. This is pt. of 400 a's granted by pat. from Fra: Lovelace dat. 19.Jun. 1671 to Thomas Lane sold to Edmonson & then to Hillyard.

Robt. Palmitary pt. of Robert's Chance 125 a. part of 500 acres granted by pat. from ye. propr. dat (none given) to Robt. Palmitary. Left by ye father among his 4 children by will.

Richd. Dawson 250 (acres) one moiety of ye above being 2 shares the one by his wife R.P.'s Daughter the other he bought of Walter Johnson who married a daughter.

Walter Johnson 125 (acres) the last share of ye abovesd. 500 a's purchased of ye youngest son having sold his wife's share to Rd. Dawson as above.

(Page 28)

James Davies for Wm. Harraway's children, 300 a's. granted by pat. they say from ye propr. dat. 1.1.84 to Cha: Jno Hillyard Junr. warrt. from Suss. Court survd. 27.9.79 Rent at Cranbrook 1 bush. per c. J. Hillyard sold this to Wm. Harraway by deed dat. 16.10.84 to whose children it belongs his wid: Susannah who married Edwd. Lowther & since James Davis. It was sold by Jno. Hillyard in 82 as per agreemt. produced but not duly survey'd to 84.

John Reynolds 200 a's. part of 400 acres call'd Intallyhay ? taken up by Jno. Galliard vid. ye entry at large pa. 30 entred there 3rd Mar. 1705/6. Jno. Galld. convd. this to Jno. Reynolds by deed dat. 10 Mar. 84 J.R. left this by will dat 10 mo. 91 to his two sons Willm. and Joseph: Joseph dying ye whole fell to Wm. who sold 200 of it to James Thomas who has since sold it to (name not given)

Will. Thomas now 200 (acres) the other moiety of ye above

Thomas Reynolds 500 (acres) taken up by Jno. Reynolds he sd. his father confirmed to him by pat. from the propr. dated (none given). J. Reynd. by will devised this to his sons John & Thomas & Thomas now holds it all.

Henry Parmain 100 (acres) part of 600 acres taken up by himself granted by pat. from ye propr. dat. 26.1.84 to Hen: Parmain warrt. blank. survd. 22.3.1680 rent at Dover 1 bushl. per c. and 1 years rent at every alienation of ye ref. Tho: Sharp holds 200 Wm. -?- 299 & Ralph Prime 100 now sold to Nich: Murphy.

(Page 29)

Jonas Greenwood part of Whitehall 600 a's., 225 a's purchased by him of Jno. Hillyard by deed dat. 7 Mar 97 being a plantation formerly in the possession of Arth. Emmery is pt. of Whitehall.

Jno. Ellet admr of Rd. Turner's estate, 200 (acres), one hund. a's. pt. thereof purchased of Jno. Bradshaw by deed dat. 15 June 98 being pt. of a tract of 300 acres then held by Jno. Bradshaw who wants a title to it. The other 100 a's purchased of Evan Jones being a deed dat 8.10.1690 being purchased by sd. Evans of Geo: Martin who took it up & was survd. by Tho: Pemberton. as per recital in ye last deed & his certif. dat. 17 Jan. 88 no pat.

Jethro Thompson Westmoreland 200 a's. laid out by Rd. Mitchell Dep: Survr. survd. 5.12.84 by a warrt. for 500 a's from Kent Court dat. 15.1.80/1 to Jno. Hillyard Junr. as per ye record of the certificate produced the tract call'd Westmoreland convey'd by J Hillyd. per acknowledgment to Jethro Thomp. 16.7. 300 a. Jethro Thomson took out a warrt. at a penny per acre for 300 a's. wch. was taken up with the other 200 per pd. rents for it as by the above rect. but he will not hold it having no pat. for it nor will accept of one.

Charles Hillyard 426 The Exchange at ye head of ye Duck Creek, more p. 27 q.v., took up by Jno. Hillyard Senr. by warrt. they say from the propr. but they cannot shew their right Charles however claims ye whole or a share.

Benjamin Gumly 800 (acres) on ye so. side of ye main branch of Duck Creek Part of a tract of 900 acres called Sherwood's Fortune alias Greenhope granted by pat. from W.M. & J. Goods. dat. 26.3.89 to Wm. Sherwood warrt. first granted by pat. from ye propr. dat. 26 Mar 84 for 400 acres ye -?- made good out of a warrt. granted to Robt. Hutchinson sold to Wm. Berry who sold to Hen: Parmain who sold to Wm. Sherwood return 9.12.84 Rent at Dover 1 bushl wheat per c. Purchased of Wm. Sherwood by B.G. 1703 of ? Turner who bought it of Wm. Sherer or Sherwood 10.10.96.

(Page 30)

Francis Wetfoodt 100 (acres) the remaining 100 of the foregoing 900 bought of Wm. Sherwood about the same time B. Gumly bought his.

B. Gumly brought over 800 (acres).

Wm. Reynolds 200 a. on ye n. side of ye western branch of Duck Creek, no name, part of a tract of 400 acres granted by pat. from ye propr. dat 26.1.84 to Jno. Galle. warrt. blank survd. 13.10.81 to J. G. is Jno. Galliard rent at Dover 1 bushl. wheat per c. & 1 years rent at every alienation.

R. Draughton Northampton, 436 a's. survd. for himself 28.9.81 by Ephr. Herman by vertue of a warrt. from St. Jones Court as per a copy the original sent up to the office for a patent.

Jos. Growdon 1000 acres granted by patent about ye year 1706 from Sr. Edmd. Andross to Fra: Whitwell for 400 a's resurvd. by Mitchel A. D. (no date given) & proved just on thousd. Resurvey'd again by Jos. Growdon in 1686 & proven about 1400 but was not returned. Surveyed by Wm. Southbe and Wm. Berry admr. to Fra: Whitwell by deed dat. 19.11.94 Jos. Growdon & by him resurvey'd about 1340 acres. Again resurvey'd by warrt. dat. 20.6.1708 & contains in ye whole 1340 acres.

Thomas Sharp 626 (acres) Divided into three parcels one of 626 a. to Thos. Sharp one of 292 a. & ye 3d 422 a's. both these two last to James Steel to wch. sd. -?- the -?- J. Growdon by deed dat. 1 & 2 of 7 1708 has convey'd ye same.

James Steele 714 a's (described above, the 292 and 422 acre tracts)

Tho. England heir of the Improvement now James Morris 600 (acres) laid out to Jno. Howel after whose decease Tho. England obtained a judgmt. against it for mony due to his wife's father from sd. Howel & ye sherif took it in Execution & for want of buyers Tho. Engd. took it for the debt and afterwds. sold it to James Morris to whom is confirmed by patent dated 12.10.1716.

SUSSEX COUNTY, DELAWARE, QUITRENTS
1702-1713

LEWES AND REHOBOTH HUNDRED

18 12TH MONTH 1705/6

Widow or David & Thomas Gray 375 acres on ye southwest side of Pagan Creek on Bever dam branch--lives on it. Warrt. to Saml. Gray from ye court 6 11 mo. 1682 survd. 2 2 mo. to ditto. Patt from ye Propr. 22 7 mo. 1701. Rent a bushl. of wheat per C. payable at Worminghurst.

More 300 below -?- they had formerly 600 acres of land of ye 300 a's. was granted by the court of Deale 13 Mar. 77/8 ye other 300 by ye same Court 8 10 mo. 1686 as of warrt. -?- 300 of which Ben Crosby 200 Timothy Dawgan 100. The above mentioned in Gray being part of the last 300 acres purchased 25 Feb. 89/90.

Timothy Dowgan 232 the other part of Saml. Gray's last tract sold by him 4 1 mo. 89 to Jno. Morris who by deed dat. 4 June 95 sold it to T. Dowgan the 32 acres it above what is contained in ye warrt. & is either overplus & to be deducted out of Gray's remainder.

Saml. Rowland 132 a's. granted to Willm. Tom by pat. from Sir Edmd. Andros dat.19 Jun 79 rent 1 bushel of wheat -?-. Luke Watson from him to Thos Wynne from his son to Sa: Rowld.

More. 150 a's. produces a draught obtained by J. -?- survd. 1693 laid out to Jonathan Wynne who sold it to him laid out about 1680 or 1682 sold to J. Wynne by Jno Jones.

More. About 100 a's. granted -?- by pat. from Gen. Fra: Lovelace dat. 2 July 1672 to Herm: Fred: Wiltbank sold to Nort: Claypoole sold by Joseph Claypoole to S. Rowland about 2 years agoe.

More. 350 granted by pat. 9 10 mo. 1691 -?-.

(Page 2)

Wm. White 457 on Love Creek called Watson's Purchase. Granted by Pat. from ye Prop dat. 30 1 mo. 84 to Luke Watson sold by Luke to Wm. White 30 8 mo. 1702 who clears it to ye line.

Isaac Wiltbank on Pagan Creek. 200 one Moiety of 400 granted by pat. from Sir Edmd. Andros dat. 25 Mar. 1676 unto Danl. Browne who sold to Saml. Preston ye whole who sold to James Peterkin who sold to Rd. Painter and Jno. Prettiman. Rd. Painter sold to Isaac.

<u>Jno. Prettyman</u> holds ye moiety of ye above.

<u>Richard Henman</u> 300 on Kings Creek part of 800 acres granted by patent Sir Edmd. Andros dat. 15 Jun. 1675 to Jno. Avery who sold about 200 to Jno. Depre whose son Jno. holds it ye other 600 he left to his daughters Mary and Jamima. Mary intermarried -?- she paid & R. Henman married her being his widow. Cap. Avery died 1682.

<u>Jno. Morgan</u> 300 The other moiety of the 600 acres left by Capt. Avery to his daughter Jamima who intermarried Jno. Morgan: he married his wife about 9 years agoe.

<u>John Depre</u> 200 sold by Capt. Avery to his father's above in R. Henman a deed dat. 10 10 mo. 72 he holds it as his heir.

More on Rehoboa granted by Pat. to Andr. Depre.

<u>Thomas Fisher</u> near Loves Creek. 400 The Prop. by his pat. dat 26 1 mo. 1684 granted to Alex. Molestine & Jno. Kipshaven 1000. Alex sold 500 to Tho: Fisher by deed dat. 8 11 mo. 1695.

<u>Adam Johnson's children</u> the other 500 Jno. Kipshaven's share came by deed of gift from her mother to his daughter Martha who married Albert Jacobs who with Wm. Clark sold it to -?-.

(Page 3)

<u>Adam Johnson's wife & Albert Jacobs children</u> 645 acres on south side of Indian River. Laid out by warrt. from Sussex court to John Barker surveyed by Joh. Barkhead 18.2.84 sold by Barker to Alb. Jacobs whose children have the right to it but the Marylanders have ousted them.

More. A tract called Kickin and Kickout about 600 a. belonged to Jno. Kipshaven grandfather to ye children Kickout was bought of Alex Molestine & Kickin of Antonio Inloss.

More. Albert Jacobs land belongs to the same children also out there is no account to be had the eldest son is near of age.

<u>Wm. Shankland</u> St. Martin on Pagan's Creek. 400 granted by pat. from Sir Edmd. Andros dat. 15 Janry. 75 to Edwd. Southeron sold to Saml. Preston by him to Wm. Shankland in 1703.

<u>James Walker</u> 400 in Angola Neck. Part of 800 acres called Webly granted by Pat. from ye Prop. as is recited in W. C.'s deed to Robt. Bracey who granted ye same excepting only the Little neck & 100 acres more is what he left to his daughter to his son Robt. Bracey who sold to Wm. Clark who by deed dat 7th mo. 1702 sold to Ja: Walker.

46

Edwd. Craig **100** purchased of Michael Chambers by deed dat. 30 9 mo. 95 when it was granted by the propr. by pat dat. 26.6.84 in a tract of 500 acres rent at Lewes 5 bushels of wheat of ye same tract he sold to Jno. Young now Jno. Willms.

More. 100 - 200 acres another 700 he also sold to ye said E. Craig by deed 5 May 1702 & holds 100.

Michael Chambers 100 the remaining 100 left unsold of the above.

(Page 4)

Jno. Williams children 200 Purchased of Mich: Chambers as noted in Edwd. Craig.

Josiah Wastecoat called Batchelors Folly 900 granted by pat. from ye prop. dat. 5 5 mo. 81 laid out ye 9 10th mo. 81 by a warrt. dat. 8.12.80 to Wm. Trotter whose attorny sold it to Wm. Clark 7th mo. 85 wh sold it by ind -?- 18th 9th mo. 1685 to Fra: Cornwell whose widow Josiah married ye land belongs to her children Francis & Mary. Rent 1 bushel per C.

More. 100 acres of marsh granted to Fra: Cornwell by warrt. dat. 10.8.85 survd. 12.4.86 contd. by pat. dat. 2.2.87 to sd. Francis. Rent one English silver penny per acre signed Ja: Clay. Mary Wastecoat complains they are -?- of her marsh by Jno. Pettyjohn.

Widow Sarah Watson 500 granted by pat dat. 26 1 mo. 84 to Luke Watson survd. 11 10 mo. next following the date of ye ordr. of court wch. is blank Luke dying his widow holds it all only that Luke sold 100 to Jonath. Graves not yet made over. Rent 5 bushels per an.

Alexdr. Molestine 96 acres part of a tract of 611 acres granted by pat. from Sir E. Andros dat. 25 Mar. 1676 to Alexandr. Molestedy rent six bushels of wheat of that there is sold to Doctr. Saml. Davies 475 a. and to Saml. Dickerson 40, 515 (acres sold).

Saml. Davies 445 bought of Pet: Lewis who bought it of Al. Molestine as above. S. Davies sold to Th: Fennwick 30 a's. & has this remaining.

More. 374 part of Bradford's entred -?- sold to Jno. Gibb who sold to Jno. Stewart whose ex. sold to S. Davies.

(Page 5)

John Crew on Rehoboa. 500 pt. of 900 acres granted by Sir Edmd. Andros by pat. dat 24 Aug. 79 to Robt. Hignat & John Crew. Jno. Crew immediately sold his interest to Robt. Hignat who sold 600 to Jno. Depre who sold 300 to Nort. Claypoole whose surveyor N. Field sold it to Fra: Cook for whom he again sold it to Crew 3.7.1700 ye other 200 he bought of Hignat 3.4.81.

Jacob Kolluck 300 part of the above purchased of Jno. Depre whose father
bought 300 acres of Hignat ye other 300 he sold to Nort: Clayp. -?- of this land
are false in ye patent J. Kolluck yfore requires a resurvey and regulation.
Owen Rock 100 ye remaindr. of the above.
Jno. West 80 in Angola Neck purchased of Wm. Clark by deed dat. 10.11.1701
being pt. of a tract (as is recited) laid out by vertue of a warrt. under the hand
and seal of Wm. Penn Prop. in a place called Angola Neck.
More. on Angola Neck 180 part of 400 acres granted by patent to Jno. Johason
ye Negro who sold ye whole to Wm. Futcher who left it to his children Eliz: &
Sarah. Jno. West married Eliz. & holds this by her. Jno. Walker married ye ot.
sister.
Jno. Roades 150 part of 550 acres granted by the propr. by pat. dat. 26 1 mo. 84
Jno. Roades his father survd. 5 2 mo. 81 ordr. of court 10 80. Rent 1 bushel of
wheat per C. His sister's husband John Henman holds the other 400.
Jno. Henman 400 the remaindr. of the above in Jno. Roades.
(Page 6)
Anderson Parker & William Spicer 600 laid out to Paul Marsh 8 of March
1680/1 by an ordr. of court. They saw he has a pat. from York now in N. Field's
office but not legible. James son of Marsh sold it to ye sd. Parker & Spicer.
Thomas Fenwick 69 granted by pat. from E. Andros dat. 15 Jan. 75 to Jno. Kipshaven who sold to Wm. Dyre who sold to T. Fenw. Rent half a bushel of wheat.
More. 67 the overplus of the above tract for which Wm. Carter of Lewes ob-
tained a warr (as is recited) from the propr. to resurvey the sd. tract & for 7:10th
sold the same to Wm. Dyre 87.
More. 36 part of the tract entred under Al: Molestine. Th: Fenwick bought this
of Peter Lewis.
Jacob Kolluck in Middle Creek Rehoboa 200 part of 400 granted by pat. from ye
prop. dat. 1 1 mo. 84 to Wm. Ematt warrt. from ye court 24.6.80 surv 27.1.81.
Rent at Lewes a bushl. of wheat per C. -?- Ematt sold Hart in 4.8.87 who sold to
Jno. Barker 200 a. who 8 mo. 98 sold to J. Kolluck 200 acres.
Abraham Molestine's children Ja. Walker, weaver 200 the remainder of ye above.
John Painter 340 part of 411 acres granted by pat. dat 25 Mar. 1676 from Sir
Edmd. Andr. to Timothy Love. Rent 4 bushls. of wheat this they inform, but he
derived from Wm. Bradford of a deed from the sd. Wm. dat. 29 July 92 to Wm.
Sweatman Peter Rayman & Roger Foret.
(Page 7)

<u>Pt. of 1200 acres called Bradford's Hall</u> 1200 acres Corbet in w he recited yt the 1200 is called Bradford Hall was granted to Nathl. Bradford by a warrt. from ye Ct. of Sussex dat. 25 Mar. 76 & confd. by ye prop. commr. by a pat. to sd. Nathl. whose son & heir conveyed as above this they say includes the former pat. from - ?- Wm. Sweatman dying gave all to his wife wth whom Rd. Painter intermarrying convey'd it to his brother Jno. Painter by deed dat 3 Feb. 1701.

<u>Richd. Painter</u> Rehoboa Peach Blossom 400 a's pt. of 900 acres called Peach Blossom on Rehoboa Bay granted by Sir Ed Andros by pat. dat. 25 Mar. 76 to Jno. King. Most of this came some way into Wm. Futcher's hand. 2 or 300 a's excepted now Fra: Richardsons at Phildia. taken by an execution Jonath: Sturges married Eliz. widow of Wm. Futcher Junr. who wth. her husb. conveyed this 400 a's by deed dat. 6 of Febr. 1704 to Rd. Painter.

<u>Morris Edwds.</u> Rehoboa Young's Hope 300 a's granted by pat. dat. 15 Jany. 75 from Edmd. Andr. to Geo. Young Rent 3 bushls. of wheat assigned 11.7.77 by G. Young to Ja: Wells on ye 10 Jan. 80 assigned by Wells to Alx. Drap. who by deed dat. 14 9 mo. 82 to Jno. Simon & N. Lowing Mor. Edwds. marrying Simon's widow hold ye whole Simons survived ye other.

<u>Nehemiah Field</u> for Nort. Claypoole 80 acres granted by pat. from Ed. Andros dat 15 Jan. 1675 to Al. Molestedy. Rent half a bushel of wheat. Sold by Al. M. to Nort. Claypoole to whose children it belongs, N. Field married their mother. More on Bundick's Branch. 500 pt. of a large tract of 1200 acres granted to Richd. Bundick who convey'd 500 a's to Nort: Claypoole. Neh. Field marrying Nort.'s admx. to pay the -?- this to Fra: Cook of Phildia. as admx. to James Claypoole. The said 1200 acres were granted by pat. from ye Propr. dat. 1 1 mo. 84 to ye sd. Rd. Bundick survey'd 3 10 mo. 80/1 rent at Lewes 1 bushl. pd. R. Bundick sold of ye above 400 more to Tho: Jones.

(Page 8)

<u>Nehm. Field</u> 300 purchased of -?- as attorney to Rd. Lawson who purchased of Jno. Cullison who took up this land before the propr. claim returned & counts 336 acres. Requests a pat.

<u>Wm Clark</u> on Broadkill 800 granted.

<u>Jonath. Baily</u> pt. of 112 acres granted w. Corn: Verhoof by pat from Sir Edmd. Andr. 29.7.77 bought of Wm. -?- aut. of -?- Pat. No. 1. Jno. Vines sheriff of Suss. by deed dat. 10.1.85 conveyed this to W. Clark for a debt recovered of Verhoof's estate at Sussex Court of 28 levied on ye sd. land & P. Groundyke of Kent ex. & admr. of Verhoof's estate released ye sd. land to sd. W. Cl. by deed dat. 23.6.86. W. Cl. by one deed dat. 26.1.85 granted on pt. of this & by another deed dat.

2.6.95 granted another pt. of ye sd. land to Jon: Baily in all about 100 acres. This
112 acres by patent called Carpenter's Yard lies at ye mouth of Whorekill Creek.
Abraham & Jno. Wiltbank 50 a's in ye town of Lewes a moiety of a grant to
Herm: Wiltbank rent 2 bushl. of wheat for ye whole the other moiety is held by
Jno. Williams.
Jno. Williams 50 a's the other moiety of the 200 a's.
(Page 9)

REHOBOA HUNDRED
Jno. Burton & Wm. Bagwell 1000 acres called Long Neck. Granted by patent
from Sir Edmd. Andros to Willm. Burton. Resurvd by a warrt from ye commr.
devised by the sd. Wm's will to his son Jno. who is seated upon it.
William Bagwell holds 500 of the above.
Wm. -?-'s children 400 acres granted by pat. dat. 29 7 mo. 1677 from Sir Ed:
Andros to James Wells. Rent 4 bushels of wheat yearly.
Richd. Bracy 200 pt. of 486 acres sold by Wm. Clark by deed dat. 8th 7 mo. 94 to
sd. R. Bracy for 55 L. & part of a tract granted to W. Cl. by pat. from ye commrs.
dat 13.7.92 to W. Cl. sold this as before. Rd. Bracy sold 286 of this to Joseph
Aylitt who holds it.
Joseph Aylit Wid: now
Jno. Cary 288 part of the above.
More. 150 Bought of Robt. Bracy in Angola Neck but is no part of the above.
More. 285 called the Horse Hand granted to Wm. Clark See ye former paymt.
to Wm. Clark, most of these lands having been his.
Wm. Symonds 200 a's part of 400 a's granted by pat. from ye comrs. dat. 1 7 mo.
1692 laid out by an ordr. of court of 1679 survd. 4 4 mo. 87 to B. N. confirmed to
Bapt. Newcomb rent 1 bushl. of wheat per. C. at ye ct. of Sussex. Bapt. New-
comb conveyed 200 a's to Wm. Symds. has had this 20 years.
Anthony Inloss' widow the other moiety of the above, they have had this 20 years.
(Page 10)
Thomas Smith 250 laid out by Corn. Verhoofe 1 Apr. 1687 as p. a draught
produced to Rd. Shoulder who dying bequeathed it to Capt. Nathl. Walker who
also bequeathed it to Majr. Dyre who by his will bequeathed it to his daughter
Mary who with her husbd Rd. Cantwell by deed dated 5 June 99 convey'd it to T.
Smith.

<u>Jno. Prettyman Junr.</u> 250 a's purchased by Jno. Prettyman Senr. of Jno. Shickbury by deed dat. 2d Mar. 96, he by deed dat. 2 7 mo. 1707 convey'd it to his son Jno. Shickb. took it up by virtue of a wart. from ye court to Rob. Richds. for 400 a's ye other 150 Tho. Pemberton holds.

<u>Aminidab Hanzer</u> 200 pt. of 400 acres granted by pat. from the propr. to Wm. Emmat dat. 26 1 mo. 84 (as pr. recital) convey'd by deed from Wm. Emmat 8 10 mo. 87 to Rd. Paynter whose widow Sarah convey'd it to Edwd. Cary & Amin. Hanzer who had it divided between ym. ye other moiety belongs to James Drake or W. Waples.

<u>Drake or Waples</u> 200 the other moiety of the above.

<u>George Marriner</u> 300 a's taken up by Capt. Avery who sold it to Jno. Sheppard whose attorney sold it to Marriner, it was taken up about 1680.

<u>Robt. Richards</u> 300 a's laid out by virtue of a warrt. in the office dat. 26 7 mo. 81 to his father Robt. Richds. and survd. about that time but never patented this lies in a small neck upon Rehoboa all vacant above it.

<u>Jno. Shackbury</u> requests 100 acres joyning on this wch. -?-.

(Page 11)

BROADKILL HUNDRED

<u>Thomas Fisher</u> 300 acres on ye south side of Broadkill. Part of 400 a's granted by patent from ye comrs. dat. 29 7 mo. 86 to Jno. Streat resurvd. 2.4.86 by a warrt. of res. 7 2 mo. 86. Rents 1 bushl. of wheat per C. Sold by Street per deed dat 8th 10 mo. 86 to Wm. Clark who by deed dat. 7 12 mo. 86 sold 300 acres to Tho: Fisher. Of ye remaindr. Jno. Fisher holds 50 a's & ye children of Abr: Potter the other 50.

More the Island. 100 convey'd by Hen: Stretcher & Jno. Millington per deed dat. 3 May 88 for 60 L to Tho: Wynne & Eliz. his wife & ye survivor their heirs etc. Eliz. Wynne by deed dated 1.12.93 granted it to Tho: Fisher and Margery his wife daughter of the sd. Eliz. & the survivor & to their heirs begotten by the sd. T. F. on ye sd. M. this war regularly takcn up. Maj. Dyre having endeavoured hard to oust F. & Mill: but their title proved so good they could not.

More. 191 pt. of Wm. Dyre -?- 1275 acres confirmed by pat. vid. -?-.

More. 500 Entered -?- to him.

<u>Elizabeth Care</u> 300 granted by pat. from J. Cl. & R. P. dat. 2 2 mo. 86 to Abr: Potter laid out (pr ye pat.) by virtue of a pat. from ye prop. dat. 26.1.84 & resurvd. 5.1.86 to A. Pottr. old renter. Rent 1 bushl. of wheat per C. at Lewes.

Ab: Potter -?- deed dat. 4 7 mo. 86 convey'd it to Jacob Warren who by deed dat
1 1 mo. 94 to Jno. Haynes who by deed dat. 2 10 mo. 95 sold it to Rob. Cade -?-.
Samuel Blundel 400 acres laid out by warrt. from ye court 5.6.82 confirmed by
pat. dat. 26 1 mo. 84 from ye propr. rent 4 bushl. at Lewes. to Jno. Street who
sold to Wm. Clark who sold it to Phil. -?- who by Ind. dat 8 12 mo. 87 convey'd it
to Mor: Edwds. who by deed dat 9.12.87 sold it to Jacob Warren whose exr. &
Bro. in law Saml. Blundel is.
More over leaf.
(Page 12)
Brought over 400 a's.
Saml. Blundel 50 pt. of 100 acres sold by Bapt. Newcomb to Abr. Potter pt of
400 acres granted by the commr. dat. 1 mo. 88. Resurvd & laid out for Bapt.
Newcomb old renter 13 2 mo. 88 confirmed by pat. from W. M. & J. Goods. dat.
3 7 mo. 89 to sd. B. N. Rent 1 bushl. of wheat per C. Bapt. N. by deed dat
15.3.91 convey'd 100 acres of this to Abr. Potter who sold this 50 acres to Jacob
Warren & ye other to Jno: Fisher.
More. Marsh 50 acres granted by warrt from ye commrs. about 94. See their
minutes for their terms.
William Newcome 200 The Propr. by pat. dat. 26 1 mo. 84 granted to Richd.
Pealy 400 acres laid out by ord. of Court dat. 19 7 mo. 75/6 survd. 7th 7 mo. 82.
Baptist Newcome Rent at Lewes 4 bushls. wheat.
Danl. Newcome 200 R. Pealy convey'd this to Bapt. Newcomb who being
posses'd of this 400 and 300 of sd. above left by his will to his sons Wm. Baptist
& Danl. Newcome 200 acres each & to Jno. Hagister ye other 100.
More among the above 4 sons. 100 granted about 12 yrs. agoe. See ye comr. min
for ye term.
Jno. Hagister 100 a. pt of Wm. Piles land purchd. of him 3 mo. 1703.
Abrah: Potter 366 part of 400 acres granted by warrt. from ye court dat. 7.12.82
to Wm. Symonds convd. by him to Corn: Johnson 20 9 mo. 85 survey'd 14.1.86 to
Cornel. & by him sold to W. Clark 3.12.86 & confirmed to sd. W. Cl. by pat from
ye commr. W.M. R.R. & J.G.dat. 6th of Apr. 1690. W. Cl. by deed convey'd this
to Jane Potter for -?- rent 1 bushl. of wheat per. c. at ye town of Sussex. W.C.
sold ye remaindr. being marsh.
More. 150 a. north side of Broadkill. Granted by pat. from W. -?- dat. 25.9.90.
Granted by ye court 15.7.86. Laid out 13.2.88 to Robt. Murdock old renter when
confirmed. Rent 1 bushl. per c. at ye town of Sussex. Convey'd by Murdock to

W. Clark & by him sold by deed dat 6 7 mo. 92 to Cha: Bright who by deed dat. 20.3.96 convey'd it to Abrah: Potter.

More. Littlefield 250 acres granted by pat. from J.Cl. & R.T. dat 2 2 mo. 86 warrt. 19.1.82 from ye court. Rent at Lewes a Bushl. of wheat per C. sold by J. Hill to Abr. Potter 300 a's.

(Page 13)

Abrah: Potter brought over 50 convey'd to Jane Potter Abraham's will by Jona. Bailey sheriff of the county by deed dat. 3.3.1703 reciting that his 100 a. pt. of 400 a;s of land & marsh granted by pat. from J.Cl. & R. T. yh. Jno. Street by deed dat. 8.9.86 sold to Wm. Clark. W. Cl. by deed dat. vid. Tho: Fisher 300. Sold this 100 to Cha: Bright & he to Joh. Rowe who dying the whole 100 (this & Jno. Fisher's was later in execution.)

More. 125, 25 more. 150 sold by W. Cl. by deed dat. 1.12.97 (as recited) to Jon: Bailey who by deed dat. 10 12 mo. 97 sold this who also purchased of Nehem: Field attorny to Jno: Haines 25 acres more pt. of a tract of 200 a's of N. Starr. J. Bailey convey'd ye whole 150 to Abr: Potter this 125 acres is pt. of 800 a's called the mill plantation entred in W. Cl's patent No. 3 surv'd 1 mo. 86.

Anthony Haverlo's children 600 a's possess'd by him from the first location as is affirmed. This has been resurv'd by a warrt. from ye   dat.   and contains they say but 440 acres is allowed to be clear'd to 1701 Wm. Clark having given a rect. in full & ye writings are burnt so that what has been overpd. is to be discount'd.

John Jones 750 a's. Tho: Molston (as by recital in another deed) had surv'd to him 4 1 mo. 1680/1 by Corn: Verhoof a tract of land called Hartfield Wood afs. & by deed dat. 8.12.86 convey'd 100 acres of it to Roger Gum. of the remaindr. he bequeathed by his will nunc. proved duly 150 acres to William Davis. Jno. Jones admr. on Davis' estate & got an execution also whom ye land according to law for his charge in maintaining his children.

Wm. Richds. 150, a pat. to W. Richds. for this without further Title producing 2 draughts) by the same nuncupative will Molston devised 100 acres to Wm. Richards and to his father Jno. Richds. 50 acres descends to the sd. Willm. who now claims 150. Wm. Clark claims ye other 200 viz. Gum's 100.

(Page 14)

Nathanl. Starr 175 acres part of 200 a's granted by pat. from ye commr. J. Cl. & R. T. dat. 14 2 mo. 87 to Rich. Patty renter survd. by order of court in 85 -?-. Rent 1 bu. per C. at Lewes. Jno. Patty his son by deed dat. 6 12 mo. 93 granted this 200 a's to Bapt. Newcomb whose excr. (as is recited) by deed dat 6 12 mo. 93 sold it to Wm. Clark who sold to Wm. Wolf who by deed dat. 20 11 mo. 95 sold it to Jno. Hains who sold to Rd. Wms. 175 a's. whose exx. sold to Nathl. Starr by deed dat. 2 Mar. 98/9.

Rowld: Parry 100 sold by Bapt. Newcomb to Rd. -?- in 85 & by him left to ye propr. by his will but being indebted to Bapt. Newcomb 18 lb. 18 s. the propr. was to de-?- so much to Newcomb for rents & then Wm. Clark sold this for ye propr. to Parry, Newcomb never having conveyed it before convey'd to Parry. More his plantation. 200 pt. of 400 granted by pat. from Sir Ed. Andros dat. 29.7.77 to Abrah: Clement Petit who sold to Hen. Stretcher who sold to Jno. Fisher & Rd. Core. Jno. Fisher left his moiety to his son Jno. who now holds it & R. Core's children hold ye other heir Parry's children in law (this by information of Fisher they have not appeared).

James Fisher 500 granted by pat. from ye propr. dat 26 1 mo. 1684 to Roger Gum survd. 8 2 mo. 82 by a warrt dat. 29.1.81. Rent at Lewes 5 bushls. R. Gum by deed dat. 10.1.85 sold this to Jno. Fisher father to ye sd. James to whom he left it by will.

More. 50 a's one moiety of 100 a's entred in Saml. Blundel bought of Abr. Potter cleared there in 1691.

More. 50 a's marsh taken up at the same home with the following.

More. 150 a's granted by pat. from ye plant. commr. dat. 24.9.1701 to Wm. Clark rent 1 bushl. at Lewes from date of survey W. Clark convey'd this to James Fisher.

Wm. Clark 800 a's on ye Broadkill south side granted to James Gray by pat. from J. Cl. & R. G. dat. by a warrt. from ye sd. commr. dat 7.2.86. Rent a bushel per C. Ja: Gray by deed dat. 6 10 mo. 87 convey'd this to Wm. Clark who has sold 500 of it to Saml. Rowland.

(Page 15)

William Fisher 1084, Given Yates Conwell 100, 984 acres. pt of 2 tracts granted in one pat. by the -?- commr. dat. 9 7 mo. 1702 to Wm. Dyer. Rent a bushl per C. from the first survey the one tract contains 400 a's ye other 175 acres -?- 275 a's. of which Tho: Fisher holds 191. This was formerly granted in a tract of 1000 acres by ye court in 81 to Nath: Walker of wch. 400 was sold & in a pat. for 400 acres to Jno. Winder dat. 20 Mar. 76. Sold by Dyer.

More. Marsh 289 acres granted to Wm. Dyre by the Commr. dat   the rent in the pat. is a penny per acre but Wm. Clark has accounted at a bushl. per C. Wm. Dyre convey'd it to Wm. Fisher.

More. Marsh 50 a's pt. of 113 acres granted by ye court per warrt. dat   survd. by Rd. Noble 20 11 mo. 81 to Jno. Richds. sold by him to Wm. Fisher by deed dat. 1.9.97 old rent on Cedar Creek.

More. Marsh 50 a's pt. of a tract of 937 granted by pat. from ye commrs. W.M., R.T. & J.G. dat. 3.8.92 to Hen Bowman Wm. Clark administrator of ye estate of H. B. Left 500-600 lbs. in debt as his deed says convey'd this 50 acres to Wm. Fhsher per deed dat. 24.11.98 this tract of 937 acres was survd. 23 1 mo. 1700/1 by virtue of a warrt from ye commrs. vid ye pat. among Wm. Clarks.

Alexander Draper 400.

Jno. Fisher 200 a. a moiety of 400 a's granted to Abra: Clemt. in Rowld. Parry pa. 14.

(Page 16)

Saml. Rowland 375 a's granted to Matthias Evertson by the court of Sussex 4 mo. 79 survey'd by Corn: Verhoof & returned by Wm. Clark into ye survie's office (as he in a certificate affirms). Matth. dying intestate his only daughter Gartreyht inherited and married Danl. Ellit who appointed & impowered Neh. Field to transfer ye sd. land to Saml. Rowld. by an instr: dat. 10 Aug. 1702 ye sd. Gartreyht having before impower'd her husband.

Ditto. 150 part of 400 acres on ye Broadkill called Swan point granted by pat dat. 4 2 mo. 88 from W.M. & J.G. to Bryan Rowles survd. by Corn: Verhoof 1 Mar. 1680/1 to sd. Bryan. Rent at Lewes 1 bushl. of wheat per C. B. Rowles convey'd 150 of this to Saml. Rowld. by deed dat. 30 Mar. 98 and 200 acres to Barns Garret & 50 to Henry Smith.

Barn Garret child: 200 part of the above pat.

More. 300 a's granted by pat. from ye propr. dat 12.4.84 to B: Garret warrt. 15.4.81 survd. 18.11.81 his children hold it. This is all ye land Garret ever held.

Henry Smith's child 50 a's part of ye above 400.

Nehemiah Field for Nort. Claypoole entred before pa. 7 80.

Wm. Piles 700 part of a tract of 800 a's granted by pat. from ye commrs. J.C. R.T. dat 19.3.86 to John Kerk first granted by pat. from Fran: Lovelace dat. 8 5 mo. 1672 to Her. Fred. Wiltbank. Rent at Lewes 1 bushl. per C. Hold of Worm. Jno. Kerk by deed dat. 10.9.88 sold this to W.P. ye other 100 Jno. Hagister holds part 2 mo. 1709.

More. 150 granted by pat dat. 26 4 mo. 91 W.M. R.T. J.C. & J.G. to Cha: Bright out 14.2.88 by ordr. of court 9.11.82 rent 1 bushl. per C. convd. by Ch. Bright per deed dat. 10.7.91 to W. Piles.

More. Marsh 50 granted by pat. from W.M. R.T. & J.G. dat. 4 Apr. 92 to Wm. Piles survd. 8.9.91 by warrt. dat. 6.2.90. Rent at ye T(own) of Sussex 1/2 a bushl.
(Page 17)
Cedar Creek or Primehook Hundred, 22 12 mo.
Al: Draper 400 in Slaughter Neck part of a tract of 1000 acres granted by patent from W.M. & J. Good. dat 22 5 mo. 89 survd. by Corn: Verhoof by ordr. of Lewes Court. Rent at Town of Sussex 1 bushl per C. Al. Draper sold 300 a's of this 10.12.87 to James Sykes of Philad. and 300 to Wm. Emmat the following year as is said. Is now held by Jno. Bennet. Al: Draper had this from his father Al: Draper by will.
Nathl. Sykes 300 pt. of the above.
Jno. Bennet 300 pt. of the above 1000 purchased of Wm. Fisher by deed dat. 4 March 1700.
Luke Watson 200 pt. of Fairfield in Primehook Neck 600 acres granted by pat. (as per recital) dat. 4.4.84 recorded at Philda. by Pat: Robisson is supposed Apr. 86. q.v. for ye rent. Rent 1 bushl. per C. at Lewes to Luke Watson Snr. who by his deed dat. 94 convey'd 200 a's of this to his son Luke.
More. Marsh on Slaughter Neck 100 a grant from ye commr not returned.
More. 775 in Primehook Neck part of 1100 acres of land granted by pat. dat. 5.1.83 to Luke Watson survd. (as per in ye deed) 24 12 mo. 84 by a special warrt. from ye propr. dat. 5 5 mo. 83. This pat. is also lost but he believes is recorded at Phildia. with the above q. vid. for the rent. Rent 1 bushel per C. Of this his brother Saml. holds 200, Tho: Crammer 50, Caleb Carwithy about 75, (total) 325.
Jno. Watson 200 pt. of the above 600 entred in Luke Watson granted to him by his father Luke Watson by deed dat. 6 10 mo. 1697.
(Page 18)
Isaac Watson 200 the remainder of this field 600 acres granted him by his father Luke by deed.
John Bellamy 1000 a. granted by pat. from T.F. & J. Clayp. dat. 1 9 mo. 84 to J. Bellamy survd. 30th 3 mo. 1684 by a warrt. from ye propr. dat 11.5.83. Rent 1 bushl. of wheat per C. at Lewes. This is now claimed both by N. Puckle & Gabr: Thomas.
Grace Richards for her son Jno. R. 300 a's part of a grant of 500 a's called Richards Purchase by patent from ye propr. dat. 1 1 mo. 84 wart. from Sus. Court 2 1 mo. 79 survd. 2 2 mo. 80 to Jno. Richards rent payable at Lewes 1 bushl. pr. J. Richds -?- left this by will to his son Jno. having first sold 100 a's to his son in law Thomas Fleming & ye other 100 to another son in law Tho: Grove.

Thomas Fleming 100 part of the above.

Thomas Grove of Kent 100 the remaindr. of ye above.

Richard Manlove 308 purchased of James Brown by deed dat. 6th of June 99 being pt. of a tract of 600 acres called Cedartown survd. to Wm. Carter & Convd. by him to Wm. Clark who sold in whole to James Brown. Ye whole tract granted by pat from ye commr. dat 29.8.86 to W. Carter wart. from Sussex Court 10th 8 mo. 81 survd. 9 1 mo. 86. Rent at Lewes 1 bushl. per C. Assignmt. Indr. 4 10th mo. 86 deed from W. Cl. to Ja: Brown dat. 4 9 mo. 90. The rest belongs to ye estate of James Brown. Jno. Man.

(Page 19)

Slaughter Creek

Thomas Tilton 300 granted by pat. from ye Propr. dated 1 4 mo. 84 to Luke Watson Junr. formerly granted by pat. from N. York to Ja: Lilly granted -?- by Sussex Court the agt. not sealing it to sd. L. Watson who has sold but not made it over to sd Thomas.

Jno. Mahon 200 a's part of 600 acres granted to Luke Watson Senr. by pat. from Tho: F. & J. Clayp. 1.3.85. warrt. 16.9.83 surv. 16.12.84. L. Watson convey'd this to Rd. Reynolds of Sussex Tho: Haselam & Jno. Mahon 200 a's each. John Mires of Lewes now holds ye other 400 a's and has the pat.

Tho: Haselam 200.

Jno. Mires 400.

Isaac Watson 1000 convd. by Wm. Clark admx of Hen: Bowman's estate for paying his debts by deed dat. 1 4 mo. 97 to John Nutter whose widow I. Wats. married. Granted to Hen: Bowman by.

Ditto entred 300 pa: 18.

Wm. Milnor 100 Purchased of Jno. Dickerson son of Jno. Dickerson by deed not executed but articles dat. 8 mo. 1708. This was taken up by Jno. Dickerson in a tract of 400 acres never patented. Wm. Milnr. desires a patent for his so being out of wch. upon making out a good warrt. & survey is to be granted. Thomas Kelly (who -?- the pt. holds 200 a's & Mark Manlove ye remaining 400).

(Page 20)

Mispmelon or Cedar Creek

Thomas May North side of Cedar Cr. Spencers Hall. 500 granted by a pat. from ye commrs. W.M. R.T. & J.Cl. da. 26 9 mo. 1690 to ye heirs & exrs. of Wm. Spencer who were Tho: May & Marg. his wife, Spencer's daughter and only child, prop. granted by patent from E. Andr. dat. 1677 -?- wch. 100 acres added by ordr. of ye chief survr. 6 3 mo. 85. Rent at ye town of Sussex 1 bushl per C.

57

Ditto. South side of Cedar Creek, 400, 500 acres granted by pat. dat. 9 7 mo. 77 to Tho: Davies from Sr. E. Andr. Rent five bushl. of wheat assigned by Tho: Davies & Indorsment 3 July 1690 to Maj. Wm. Spencer whose adm. T. May & his wife are. T. May complains that W. Cl. cutt of 100 a's of this land so that he holds but 400 but craves a resurvey. This grant was void by N. York laws & afterwds. taken up for Hen: Pennington of whom it was purchased but ye York was being most favourable in ye bounds T.M. is willing to stand by that but by it he interferes with his neighbors.

Willm. Stapleton 400 a's part of Wm. Darval's tract of 700 a's purchased of Jno. Richards in deed dated   who purchased of Wm. Peck who took it in execution for a debt due to Jno. Vines. See ye entry of 100 acres to Jno. Waltham for this & ye following Pa. 23.

Thomas Stapleford 200 part of the same tract purchased also of Jno. Richards who was possessed of the whole 700 acres ye other 100 was convey'd by T. Stap: to Jno. Waltham. See ye above.

Jno. Manlove Pt. of Hart's Delight. 167 part of 600 acres call'd Harts Delight granted by pat. from ye propr. dat   to Robt. Hart, Senr. Purchased of Hen: Molleston by deed who purchased of Sa: Jennings ye whole 600 a's who purchased it of Robt. Hart.

Tho. Clifton holds of this   412
Jn. Harrison   42
-?- 21 acres.

Tho: Clifton 400 or 412 purchased about 10 years agoe of Hen: Molleston who is to clear ye rents. Part of the above tract.

(Page 21)

Jno. Wheeler 200 a's purchased of Hen: Molleston but not made over part of 500 acres granted by recital in Ja: Jankins deed by pat. from W.M. R.T. & J.G. dat 1 12 mo. 93/4 to Wm. Clark who by deed dat 9 Mar. 94/5 convey'd 200 a's of it to James Johnson who by deed dat. 16 Apr. 95 conv. it to Tho: Clifton who by deed dat 1 June 96 convey'd it to Hen: Moleston who sells to J. Wheeler.

Art Verkirk Bald Eagle Point 800 a's part of a tract of   acres granted by pat. from W.M. R.T. & J.G. dat. 3.8.92 to Hen: Bowman whose adm. W. Cl. to pay debt by deed dat. 24.11.98 convey'd 100 a's to Art Verk: This tract they say was purchased of Th. Skidmore & Tho. Williams for 500 acres but here is about 900 old out of it.

Item. His plantation 300 a's part of 700 acres sold to him by Wm. Cowdery 11 10 mo. 81 but not duly convey'd ye other 400 were sold to Tho: May & he procured a pat. for it with 100 acres added entred per his pat., the title is ye same wch. that of Mays, originally ye whole was 700 a's taken up by Josias Cowdery whose brother & heir sold it as before.

Thomas Joyce children Kingston 119 a's part of the 500 acres mentioned in Jno. Wheeler. Wm. Cl. by recital in this deed of his mentions it that it was at first laid out to Geo: Cullen who sold it to Jno. Edmundson who sold it to W. Clark who by deed dat. 12 June 97 convey'd this to Tho: Joyce.

Thomas Grove for Henry Smith's son Jno. Smith the Delight in Primehook Neck 600 a's granted by pat. from ye propr. 5.5.83 surve. 5.3.84. Held of Worminghurst. Rent at Lewes 1 Bushl. of per C. T. Grove married Hen: Smith's widow about 13 yrs. agoe.

Tho. Grove the Choice 400 a's granted by pat. from ye commrs. J.Cl. & R.T. dat. 24.6.85 to Wm. Wargent warrt. from the propr. dat. 13.12.84 survd. 13.5.85 to Wm. Wargt. Rent at Lewes 1 bushl. per C. Wm. Wargt. by deed dat. 8 10 mo. 85 convey'd this to Sarah Godsel the psent wife to T. Grove relict also of Hen: Smith.

Ditto. ye Hazard 400 a's granted by pat. from J.Cl. & R.T. dat 24 6 mo. 85 to Bapt. Newcomb warrt. in Lewes from (Page 22) the court of Sussex dat. 14.5.85 survd. 27 5 mo. 85 to sd. Bapt. Newc: Rent at Lewes 1 bushl. per C. Convey'd by Bapt. Newcomb by deed dat. 8 10 mo. 85 to sd. Sarah Godsel now wife of Tho. Grove.

Tho: Grove 418 pruchased of Wm. Dyre by deed dated 6th Mar. 98/9 in part of Maj. Dyre's tract taken up for 1000 acres of wch. he convey'd ye other 600 acres to Wm. Fisher.

Marsh about 750 granted by warrt. from the commrs. & survd. by Th: Pemb. sent up ye certificate to J.L. He says to get a pat.

Gabriel Henry 400 purchased by him of Hendr. Gravens by deed dat. 27th of Aug. 97 being pt of a tract called Bowmans Farm laid out for (as they say) about 500 a's to Jno: Wooteon who sold to Hen: Bowman by pat. in -?-.

Jno. Abbot holds of ye same tract 200.

& Wm. Hedget   136.

Joseph Hickman 200 a's purchased of Hen: Bowman by deed dat. 2 10 mo. 93 being pt of a tract call'd Bowman's Farm, this is part of a tract of 3000 acres as they inform. Of this tract Jno. Watson holds 1000 a's entred pa. 19. Thos: Davies 800 a's lives on it.

Nicholas Granger Granger's Field 250 part of a tract per recital in the deed granted by warrt. from Sussex County to Robt. Hudson, made over by R. Hudson to Hen: Bowman who in his life time sold this to N. Granger but having never convey'd it. N.G. have a deed for it price L 62:10/ dat. 5.11.'98. By that warrt. there was 450 a's taken up is of ye same they say entred in Art Verkirk. Eliz. Cade 200 Eliz: Cade holds ye other 200. S. Preston & Hen. Wallowe to clear it. No pat. survd. about 93 they say & ye title bad.

Thomas Wilson 200 a's part of a tract of 425 a's called Callis Land granted by pat. from J.Cl. & R.T. as per W. Cl's recital dat. 29 7 mo. 86 to Hen: Pennington who by deed dat 14 7 mo. 86 convey'd it to Wm. Clark who sold it to Tho: Wynne Archbd. Mickle (Page 23) & Jno. Low ye two last of wch. having only one moiety appointed W. Clark their attorny who by deed dat. 6.10.97 convey'd it to Tho: Wilson Josh: Cowdry has ye other part.

James Seaton ye mill 50 a's purchased of Jos: Booth who bought this of W. Clark to build a mill on & is pt of a tract granted to Hen: Bowman.

Thomas Manlove 350 bought of Hen. Bowman in his life time as per his bond to make a title dat 13 June 93. No title ever made either by him of Wm. Clark is part of Skidmore's patent.

Jno. Waltham 297 purchased in two parcels one of 200 a's convey'd to him by Hen: Bowman by deed dat 14.3.1691 reciting but his part of a tract of land purchased by H. Bowman of Th. Skidmore and Tho: Williams commonly call'd of the Gravesent reputed to contain 700 acres but being resurvey'd by virtue of a special warrt. from ye propr. commissionrs. 9th of Aug. 1690 by taking in points was mode up 933 acres. Confid. 50 lbs. The other tract of 97 acres purchased by Jno. Wathm. of Wm. Clark by deed dat. 1st of June 1700. pt of ye same tract above but this deed recites that his part of 933 a's granted by pat. to Hen: Bowman from W.M. R.T. & J.Cl. dat. 9th of Aug. 90 ye same day wch. the warrt. above wch. cannot be confid. 35 lbs.

Item. 100 a's part of 700 acres laid out 21 Janry. 1681 to Rob. Hart Senr. convd. by him to Wm. Darval upon whose estate Wm. Emmat exr. of Jno. Vines obtain'd a judgemt. & execution for 11 lbs. wch. was levied on this 700 a's being appraised at 42 lbs. but none buying it was exposed to sale it was again exposed by Jno. Hill & purchased for 37 lbs. by Will: Clark who engaged to clear ye rents & then sold it to Jno. Richards who sold 400 a's to Wm. Stapleton & 300 a's to Tho: Stapleford who by deed dat. 1.6.1704 for 15 lbs. sold this 100 a's to J. Waltham.

Joseph Booth 400 a's part of a tract of 1000 a's granted by pat. from Sir. Edm: Andros dat. 29 7 mo. to Rd. Hill called Hill's Content convey'd to Benj: Cowdery by deed dat. 7 July 88. B.C. by deed of gift granted to his daughter Frances

Spencer Maj. Wm. Spencer's wife 500 a's pt. of this & ye other 500 a's to Henry Spencer & Samuel Spencer & confirmed to ye sd. Fra: Spencer to hold 500 a's to her & her heirs etc. & ye other 500 a's to sd. Hen. & Wm. Spencer their excrs heirs etc. by one pat. from ye commrs. W.M. R. T. & J.Cl. dat. 8th of 8 mo. 90. Rent at ye town of Sussex 1 bushl. per C. J. Booth married Frances Spencer and holds in her right.

Saml. Spencer 250 part of the above he purchased 100 acres of his sisters land being ye remaindr. of ye 500 acres of his mothers share & sold his brother 100 of his part.

Hen: Spencer 350 the complemt. of ye 1000 a's made up of his own 250 & 100 bought of his brother.

James Brown

(Page 25)

Broadkill

at his house 23 12 mo. 1705/6

John Hill Branston his dwelling house 430 a's granted by pat. from J.Cl. & R.T. dated 1 3 mo. 85 to himself warrt. from Sussex Court 12 7 mo. 82 survd. 11 12 mo. 84. Rent 1 bushl.wheat per C.

Marsh. 50 a's granted by pat from J.Cl. & R.T. dated 1.3.85 to himself warrt. from Ye propr. 16.6.84 survd. 11 12 mo. 84. Rent blank allowed at a bushl per C.

600 a's granted by pat. from Sir. Edmd. Andr. dated 20 Aug. 1679 to Tho: Howard & Knight Howard. Rent six bushls. of wheat per an. Purchased by Jno. Hill partly of Howard & partly of L. Watson his exr. but ye title not made.

Ye Point. 250 granted by pat from ye commrs. -?- dated 10 7 mo. 1702 to Jno. Hill by a warrt from ye propr. dat. 25.8.1701. Rent 1 bushl. of wheat per C. payable from ye 1st of March 1686 at Lewes.

In ye forrest 650 granted by pat. from W.M. & J.Cl. dated 5 6 mo. 87 to Tho: Tilton warrt. from Sussex court 16 12 mo. 81 survd. 13 12 mo. 86. Rent 1 bushl. per C. at Lewes. Tho: Tilton by deed dat 4.1.95 convd. this to Hen: Bowman whose adm to pay his debts convey'd it to Jno. Hill by deed dat. 15.10.96.

Cornelius Wiltbank 150 a's part of 1100 a's granted to Jno. Winder pt. of Wm. Dyer's tract sold them in 95 & again confirmed by deed dat 8.3.1707 this is part of W. Dyre's 2100 a's on South Broadkill. 212 1/2 one moiety of 425 a's granted by patent from ye prop dat 1 1 mo. 84 to Hermannus Wiltbank wart. from Sussex Court 15 1 mo. 82 survd. 1 1 mo. 82. Rent at Lewes 1 bushl. per C. Cornelius ye

61

eldest son holds this half & his brother Abrah: & Isaac ye other moiety now sold to Saml. Rowland.

Saml. Rowld 212 1/2 the other moiety.

(Page 26)

Jno. Dunnavan 234 1/2 one moiety of 469 acres granted by pat. from ye propr. dat. 1 1 mo. 84 to Hermanus Wiltbank war. from Sussex Court blank survd. 9 1 mo. 81. Rent 1 bushl. of wheat per C. at Lewes. Half of this came to Corn. Wiltbank Herm's eldest son who sold it to Cha: Bright who sold to Jno. Dunnavan but Wiltbank convey'd it to Dunnavan. Abrah. & Is. Wiltbank hold ye ote. moiety.

Abrah: & Is: Wiltbank 234 1/2 the other moiety of the above.

Jno. Bennet 200 purchase.

-A-
ABBOTT, John, 59
ABERDEEN, 37
ABRAMS, John, 11
ALBERTSON, John, 20
ALBURNE, 1
ALBURTON, John, 1
ALFORD, John, 1
ALLEN, William, 1
ALLIN, Samson, 24
ALLIT, Joseph, 28
ALLOM CABIN, 42
ALLOM'S CABIN, 41
ALLSTONE, Arthur, 21
ALLUM'S CABIN, 40
ALMAN, Joseph, 18
ALRICHS, Hermanus, 11
Jacobus, 10
Peter, 11
Sigfridus, 11
ALSTON, Arthur, 40
ANDERSON, Erick, 13
James, 15
Rowlif, 18
Urin, 15
ANDREE, Widow, 18
ANDREW, Daniel, 7
ANDROS, E., 36, 37, 47, 48
Ed, 49
Edmond, 32, 38, 45, 46, 47, 50, 60
Edward, 54
ANDROSS, Edmond, 44
ANGELL FORD, 6
ANGLEFIELD, 3
ANGLETON, 2
ANGOLA NECK, 48, 50
ANNAND, W., 34
APPACONIE, 4
ARUNDELL, 1, 7
William, 7
ASHAM, Jonas, 14
ASHTON, Robert, 17
ASKUE, John, 29

ATKIN, James, 28
ATKINS, Sampson, 17
Timothy, 16
William, 28
ATTHOW, Thomas, 38
AUSBOG, 3
AVERY, Capt., 51
Jamima, 46
John, 7, 46
Mary, 46
AYLITT, Joseph, 50

-B-
BAGGWELL, Widow, 27
BAGWELL, William, 50
BAILEY, Jonathan, 53
BAILY, Jon:, 50
Jonathan, 49
BAKER, Ambrose, 12
James, 12
BALD EAGLE POINT, 58
BALEY, Jonathan, 27
BALL, John, 18
William, 14, 19
BARBER, Robert, 28
BARK, 6
BARKER, John, 7, 27, 46, 48
William, 25
BARKHEAD, John, 46
BARKIN, 9
BARKINTON, 2
BARKSTEAD, Joshua, 1, 37
BARKSTEAD HAZZARD, 4
BARNES, Garret, 7
John, 1, 21, 23, 25, 34
BARNS, Paul, 11
BARRON POINT, 3
BARSNET, Richard, 25
BARTLET, Jane, 1
Nicholas, 1, 34
Richard, 1
BARTLETS LOT, 1

BASNET, Richard, 22
BATCHELORS FOLLY, 47
BATTEN-BOROUGH, Anthony, 12
BATTY, Robert, 18
BAWCOMB, Peter, 1
BAYLEY, Richard, 1
BAYNTON, Peter, 16
BEACHAM, Richard, 16
BEAR GARDEN, 2
BEDFORD, Thomas, 14
BEDLLAMY, John, 56
BEDWELL, Henry, 33
John, 1
Robert, 1, 24, 31, 32, 33
Thomas, 23, 26, 32, 34, 35, 38
BELLAMY, John, 7
BENING, Christopher, 18
BENNET, John, 56, 62
BERRY, THE, 8
BERRY, Samuel, 37
William, 35, 38, 39, 43, 44
BERRY'S RANGE, 38
BESERT, Thomas, 27
BESSANT, Thomas, 7
BEST, Humphrey, 11
BETTON, Francis, 20
BETTS, John, 1, 31, 40
Robert, 4, 30, 39
BIGGS, John, 2
BILLINGATE, 6
BISHMORE, John, 19
BISHOP, B., 34
Benjamin, 33
Benoni, 33
Benony, 1
Henry, 1
Margaret, 33
BISHOP'S CHOICE, 33
BISK, John, 10
BLACKMAN, Henry, 12

BLACKSMITHS HALL, 8
BLAKE, Edward, 11
BLANCHARD, John, 10
BLOOMSBERRY, 6
BLUNDEL, Samuel, 52, 54
BOLTON, John, 18
BOOTH, Frances, 61
 J., 61
 Joseph, 27, 60
BOSNE, Michael, 1
BOSTOCK, Thomas, 2, 7, 40
BOTESMAN, Urin, 13
BOURDAT, Samuel, 41
BOURDET, Peter, 41
BOURNE, 8
BOWLSTOCK, Thomas, 21
BOWMAN, Henry, 1, 7, 26, 28, 55, 57, 58, 59, 60, 61
 John, 33
 Margaret, 33
BOWMAN'S FARM, 59
BOWMANS FARM, 7, 59
BOWMANS FARMS, 7
BOYER, Dr., 33
 John, 33
BRACEY, Robert, 27, 46
BRACY, Richard, 50
 Robert, 7, 50
BRADFORD, 47
 Nathaniel, 49
 William, 7, 48
BRADFORD'S HALL, 49
BRADFORDS HALL, 7
BRADSHAW, John, 1, 20, 43
BRADSHAW'S BERRY, 1

BRADSHAWS CHOICE, 4
BRADY, B., 39
 Benjamin, 39
BRANING, Edward, 17
BRANSCOMB, Thomas, 26
BRANSTON, 8
BREWERTON, Samuel, 17
BREWSTER, John, 14
BRIDGETOWNE, 5
BRIDGEWORTH, 37
BRIGGS, John, 36
BRIGHT, Charles, 7, 53, 55, 62
BRINCKLOE, John, 22, 26, 30, 31, 36, 37
BRINKLOE, Capt., 37
 John, 36, 39
 William, 35, 37
BRINKLOW, John, 1
BRINKLOW'S GIFT, 1
BROADBERRY, Peter, 17
BROADKILL, 49
BROCKNOCK, 3
BROOKS, John, 1
BROWN, Daniel, 31
 James, 29, 57, 61
 John, 29
 William, 14
BROWNBURY, 8
BROWNE, Daniel, 25, 31, 45
 Daniell, 1
BRYAN, Robert, 13
BRYER, John, 28
BUCKLY, John, 16
BUGBEY, Richard, 23
BUNDICK, Richard, 49
BURBARY, Samuel, 22
BURBERRY, Samuel, 34, 35
BURBERRYS BERRY, 2

BURBERY, Samuel, 1, 31, 32
BURFORD, John, 18
BURGRAVE, John, 19
BURKILL, Joseph, 28
BURROUGHS, Edward, 34
BURROWS, William, 18
BURTON, Cesar, 29
 John, 1, 22, 36, 37, 50
 Robert, 27
 Robert French, 36
 Timothy, 29
 William, 27, 50
BURTONS, 37
BURTON'S DELIGHT, 35, 36
BYARD, Peter, 18
BYFIELD, 37

-C-
CADE, Elizabeth, 60
 Robert, 52
CADES DELIGHT, 8
CALLIS LAND, 60
CAMBELL, Thomas, 22
CANN, John, 11
CANNON, Urias, 25
CANTWELL, Mary, 50
 Richard, 50
CARE, Elizabeth, 51
CARPENTER, James, 29
CARPENTER'S YARD, 50
CARRON, Thomas, 40
 Timothy, 21
CARTER, William, 7, 48, 57
CARWITHY, Caleb, 56
CARY, Edward, 51
 John, 50
CEDARTON, 7
CEDARTOWN, 57

CHAMBERS,
Michael, 47
 Mikel, 28
CHAMPION, John, 14
CHANCE, 1
 Alexander, 2, 22
CHANT, John, 22
CHART, John, 35
CHASFORD, 5
CHEAT, THE, 9
CHEATE, John, 41
CHILD, Thomas, 13
CHIPPIN NORTON,
39
CHOICE, 59
CHOYSE, 10
CLAR, William, 60
CLARK, John, 12, 24
 W., 38, 49, 52, 53, 59,
60
 Whorekill, 39
 William, 2, 7, 25, 26,
30, 31, 46, 47, 48, 49,
50, 51, 52, 53, 54, 55,
57, 58, 60
CLARKE, William, 33
CLARKS, William, 55
CLAWSON, Jacob, 12
CLAY, Ja:, 47
CLAYPOOLE,
James, 11, 49
 Joseph, 45
 Nort., 47, 49, 55
 Nort:, 45
 Norton, 2, 7
CLAYTON, 4
 James, 21, 36
 John, 22, 33, 37
 Joseph, 11
 Joshua, 33
 Mary, 34
CLEMENT,
Abraham, 7
CLEMENTS, Jacob,
15
CLEMT., Abraham, 55
CLIFFORD, George,
2, 22
 John, 40
 Thomas, 2, 21, 37, 40
CLIFTON, Mikel, 28

 Robert, 26, 30
 Thomas, 58
 thomas, 29
CLIFTONS HALL, 7
CLOUD, Joseph, 16
CLOWD, Jeremiah, 16
 John, 16
COCK, John, 15
COCKHILL, 35
COLE, Edward, 12
COLLICK, Jacob, 27
COLUMN, 33
CONCORD, 35, 39
CONSTANTINE,
Conrade, 15
CONTENT, THE, 39
CONWELL, Yates, 54
COOK, Francis, 47, 49
 George, 11
 Niel, 13
COON, Thomas, 17
COOPER, James, 2
 Samuel, 2, 5
COOPERS HALL, 2
COOPERSBURY, 2
COPE, Olliver, 16
CORBET, 49
CORBITT, R., 26
CORE, Richard, 54
CORNBERRY, 9
CORNHILL, 9
CORNWALL, 5
CORNWELL,
Francis, 47
 Mary, 47
CORTLAND,
Stephanusvan, 7
CORWALL, Francis, 7
COURSEY, David, 7
COURTNEY, John, 2,
22, 32
COURTNY, ---, 32
 Robert, 14
COUTTS, James, 33
COVERDEL,
Thomas, 29
COWDERY, Ben-
jamin, 60
 Frances, 60
 Josias, 59
 William, 58

COWDRY, Joshua, 60
COWLSON, George,
16
COX, Richard, 28
CRAIG, E., 47
 Edward, 47
CRAMER, Thomas, 28
CRAMMER, Thomas,
56
CRANBROOD, 32
CRANBROOK, 31,
33, 39, 42
CRAPP, Walter, 14
CRAVEN, John, 20
CRAWFORD,
Richard, 17
CREW, John, 29, 47
CROPPER, John, 2, 7
CROSBY, Ben, 45
CROSEE, William, 11
CROSLEY, Ben, 28
CROSTOWNE, 7
CUDWITHE, Collins,
29
CULLEN, George, 2,
59
CULLIN, cornelius, 24
 George, 25
CULLISON, John, 49
CURTIS, Caleb, 32
 John, 2, 24, 30, 32
 Richard, 25
CURVEHORN, Laci,
16

 -D-
DABBS, B., 34
 Benjamin, 34, 35
DANIEL RUTTY'S
TRACT, 32
DARBY, Daniel, 7
 John, 17, 19
DARRINGTON,
William, 2
DARVAL, William,
38, 58, 60
DARVALL, William,
38
 william, 23
DAVID, Will, 29
DAVIDS, John, 29

Will, 28
DAVIDS BERRY, 2
DAVIES, Evan, 39, 41
 James, 42
 Samuel, 47
 Thomas, 58, 59
DAVIS, James, 14, 42
 John, 2
 Thomas, 29
 William, 53
DAWGAN, Timothy, 45
DAWSON, Richard, 42
 Widow, 29
DE WITT, Marinus, 17
DEAN, Peter, 12
DEHAES, Johannes, 10
 Roeloff, 10
DELIGHT, 59
DEMBRICK, Edward, 28
DEMPSEY, Daniel, 2
DENBIGH, 35, 37
DEPRE, Andrew, 46
 John, 46, 47, 48
DEPREE, Andrew, 7
 Jacob, 28
 John, 28
DERBY TOWNE, 6
DERINGH, Matthias, 11
DERVALL, William, 2
DEVOS, Matthias, 13
DICKERSON, John, 57
 Samuel, 47
 William, 22
DICKSON, William, 2
DIEWETT, Morgan, 16
DITCHERS HALL, 10
DIXON, John, 7
 William, 15
DIXONS BERRY, 7
DOBSON, Richard, 29
DODD, Abell, 17
DONAHO, Michael, 24

DONALDSON, John, 10
DONAVAN, John, 29
DONOHOE, Michael, 38
DOUNJON, Timothy, 28
DOVER, 32
DOVER FARMS, 38
DOVER RIVER, 38
DOWGAN, Timothy, 45
DOWNES, THE, 5
DRAKE, James, 51
DRAPER, Al., 56
 Al:, 56
 Alexander, 2, 7, 55
 John, 29
 Widow, 29
DRAPERSBURY, 2
DRAREY, Richard, 28
DRAUGHTON, R., 44
 Robert, 20
DUBOIS, John, 34
DUNN, John, 12
DUNNAVAN, John, 62
DURELL, Timothy, 23
DYER, Robert, 13
 William, 54, 61
DYRE, Maj., 51
 Majr., 50
 Mary, 50
 W., 61
 William, 26, 48, 51, 54, 59

-E-
EACH, Tomas, 16
EDENTON, 37
EDINGTON, 4
EDMONDS, Robert, 23, 33
EDMONDSON, 42
EDMUNDS BERRY, 1
EDMUNDSON, John, 59
EDMUNSON, John, 2
EDWARDS, Mor., 49

Mor:, 52
Morris, 27, 49
ELKS HORNE, 2
ELLET, John, 43
ELLINSWORTH, William, 2
ELLIS, John, 14
ELLIT, Daniel, 55
 Gartreyht, 55
EMATT, William, 48
EMERSON, Elizabeth, 40
 Jacob, 33
 Vincent, 39
EMLY, Luke, 13
EMMAT, William, 2, 51, 56, 60
EMMATT, William, 28
EMMERY, Arthur, 43
EMMET HALL, 8
EMPSON, Cornelius, 15
ENGLAND, Joseph, 18, 19
 Thomas, 39, 44
ENGLD, T., 37
ENLOES, Anthony, 27
ERICKSON, Erick, 12
ERIXON, Matthias, 17
EUSTASON, Lawrence, 13
EVANS, John, 23, 36
EVERET, John, 33, 35, 36
 Thomas, 22
EVERETT, Mark, 23
EVERSON, Mathias, 7
EVERTSON, Gartreyht, 55
 Henry, 12
 Matthias, 55
EXCHANGE, (THE), 42, 43

-F-
FAIRFIELD, 2, 7, 56
FARMERS DELIGHT, 9
FARRAN, Thomas, 29
FARWELL, John, 29

FENWICK, Th., 47
Thomas, 48
FIELD, Nehemiah, 28, 49, 53, 55
FINCH, John, 7
FINCHES HALL, 7
FINLOE, Alexander, 16
FISHER, Ad., 32
Ad:, 31
Adam, 24, 31
James, 54
John, 29, 51, 52, 53, 54, 55
Margery, 51
Thomas, 26, 46, 51, 53, 54
William, 54, 55, 56, 59
FITZGERRARD,
James, 36
Mary, 40
FLEMING, Thomas, 56, 57
FLOWER, Thomas, 2
FLOWERFIELD, 2
FLOWERS, John, 35
Thomas, 23
FLOWERS' LOTT, 39
FLOWERY NECK, THE, 1
FOLLY NECK, 32
FORAT, John, 10
FORET, Roger, 48
FOSTEGUE, John, 23
FOSTER, John, 40, 41, 42
FOUNTAIN, 9
FOX, John, 29
FRAMTON,
Elizabeth, 2
Widow, 2
William, 2, 3
FRANCIS, Robert, 3
FRANKLIN, Thomas, 28
FREDERICK, Edward, 3
FREELAND, 30
Isaac, 22
William, 21
FREEMAN, W., 31

William, 2, 24, 25, 30, 31
FREEMANS RANGE, 2
FREITH MANNR., 39
FRENCH, John, 41
R., 35, 37
Robert, 35, 36
FRITH MANOR, 37
FUTCHER,
Elizabeth, 48, 49
Sarah, 48
William, 48, 49

-G-
GALLE., John, 44
GALLIARD, John, 42, 44
GARDNER, John, 13
GARLAND, Silvester, 11
GARRET, Barns, 55
GARRETSON,
Henry, 14
John, 13
Paul, 14
GARRISON, John, 13
GARRITT, Barnes, 27
GARVEY, Owen, 23
GARVIE, Owen, 33
GAVESEND, 4
GENNEFELLS,
Thomas, 21
GIBB, John, 47
GIBBON, Edmond, 3
Francis, 3
GIBBONS' POINT, 32
GIBBS, Edward, 17
GILBERT, John, 30
GILL, Richard, 28
GILLOM, Robert, 3
GLASS, Arthur, 27
GLOVER, Elizabeth, 36
John, 3, 35
Mary, 36
Richard, 3, 35
GODDIN, Daniel, 35
GODIN, Peter, 12
GODSEL, Sarah, 59
GOGIN, David, 34

GOLAM, 8
GOLD, Edward, 29
GOLDEN BOWER, 7
GOLDEN MINNE, 5
GOLDEN QUARTER, 7
GOLDEN RIDGE, 1
GOLDEN THICKET, 6
GOLDSMITH, William, 29
GONSALES, Thomas, 41
GONSALEZ,
Thomas, 41
GOOD, J., 56
GOODS, J., 30, 43, 52
W. M., 43
GOOSBERRY, 3
GOOSBERY, 6
GOOSEBERRY, 30
GOSBERRY, 8
GRADINGTON, 3
GRADY, Patrick, 3
GRAIM, Thomas, 18
GRANGER, N., 60
Nicholas, 29, 59
GRANGER'S FIELD, 59
GRANHAM, John, 14
GRANT, Alexander, 29
William, 19
GRAVENS, Hendr., 59
GRAVES, John, 28
Jonathan, 47
Samuel, 28
GRAVESENT, 60
GRAY, David, 45
James, 7, 54
Samuel, 30, 45
Samuell, 27
Thomas, 45
Widow, 45
GREAT GENEVA, 39
GREAT PIPE ELM, 36
GREEN, Edward, 14
Matthew, 24

GREENE, William, 3, 20
GREENFIELD, 4, 7
GREENHOPE, 43
GREENWAY, 3
GREENWICH, 2
GREENWOOD, John, 42
Jonas, 38, 43
Jones, 40
GRIFFIN, Richard, 11
GRIGG, John, 13
GROENENDICK, Peter, 23
GROENENDIK, Peter, 6
GRONENDIK, Peter, 3
GROUNDIKE, Peter, 31
GROUNDYKE, P., 49
GROVE, Sarah, 59
T., 59
Thomas, 3, 56, 57, 59
GROVES, Thomas, 26
GROWDON, Joseph, 3, 20, 44
GRUBB, John, 16, 19
GUEST, William, 15
GULICK, Yoakam, 8
GUM, Roger, 54
GUM., Roger, 53
GUMLY, B., 44
Benjamin, 43
GUPTON, William, 34

-H-
HAGGISTER, John, 8
HAGISTER, John, 52, 55
HAINES, John, 53
HAINS, John, 54
HALES, John, 11, 17
HALL, Charles, 8
John, 31, 40
Lod:, 40
Robert, 24, 40
Thomas, 8
HALLYWELL, Richard, 10

HAMAR, Henry, 29
HAMBLY, Richard, 17, 20
HANGER, Aminidab, 28
HANS, John, 15
HANSON, Hans, 17
Timothy, 41
HANZER, Aminidab, 51
HARKLES PLAINS, 8
HARLAND, George, 13
HARMERSON, John, 29
HARMS, Katherine, 10
HARRAWAY, Susannah, 42
William, 42
HARRISON, Edward, 12
Jn., 58
HART, 48
George, 24, 34, 35, 36
Robert, 8, 58, 60
HARTFIELD WOOD, 53
HART'S DELIGHT, 58
HARTS RANGE, 8
HARVEY, Richard, 28
HARWOOD, Patrick, 22
HASELAM, Thomas, 57
HASSARD, 8
HASSOLD, Thomas, 4
HAVERLA, Anthony, 28
HAVERLO, Anthony, 53
HAY, Adam, 12
HAYN, Artman, 12
HAYNES, Charles, 29
John, 52
HAZARD, 59
HEALLY, John, 17
HEATH, James, 28

HEATHER, Thomas, 3, 23
HEATHERD, Thomas, 3, 25
HEDGET, William, 59
HENDRICK, John, 13
HENMAN, John, 48
Richard, 46
HENRIKSON, Arnd., 41
HENRY, Gabriel, 59
HERMAN, Casparus, 19
Ephr., 32, 44
HEWS, James, 18
HEYFIELD, 6
HICKMAN, Joseph, 29, 59
HIGH CROSS, 4
HIGNAT, ---, 48
Robert, 47
HILBURNE, 3
HILL, J., 53
John, 4, 8, 26, 60, 61
Richard, 60
Samuel, 22
Thomas, 4
William, 4
HILLIARD, ---, 40
Charles, 3
John, 3, 39, 42
Joseph, 33
Oliver, 3
Thomas, 3
HILLINGTON, 3
HILL'S ADVEN-TURE, 4
HILL'S CONTENT, 60
HILLYARD, 41
Charles, 20, 42, 43
Charles John, 42
J., 42
John, 20, 25, 37, 40, 42, 43
Oliver, 42
HILLYARDS, John, 41
HILLYARDS AD-VENTURE, 37

HILTON, 3
HIRONS, Elizabeth, 35
Francis, 35, 36
S., 36
Simon, 21, 35
HODGES, Barnet, 4
HOGBIN, Richard, 25, 26
HOGG, George, 10
HOGGISTER, John, 4
HOLLAND, 3
Richard, 3
HOLLINGSWORTH, Henry, 16
Thomas, 16
Valentine, 16
HOLLIWAY, Richard, 29
HOLLY NECK, 33, 34
HOLME, Thomas, 31
HOLT, John, 12
HORFFORD, George, 3
HORSE HAND, 50
HOW, John, 28
HOWARD, Knight, 61
Thomas, 61
Wights, 29
HOWE, John, 18
William, 18
HOWEL, John, 39, 44
HOWELL, John, 23
HOWELLS LOT, 6
HOWELS' LOTT, 39
HOWLING QUARTER, 5
HUDDEN, Richard, 17
HUDSON, Robert, 4, 23, 33, 59
HUGGINS, Cornelus, 12
Francis, 20
HUMFRY, Alexander, 3
HUMPHREY, Ellis, 17
HUNTING QUARTER, 6

HUTCHINSON, Robert, 13, 43

-I-
IMPROVEMENT, 4, 44
IMPROVEMENT ON DUCK CREEK, 39
INGLEBOROUGH, 3
INLOES, Abraham, 10
INLOSS, Anthony, 50
Antonio, 46
INTALLYHAY, 42
IRON, Simon, 39
IRONS, Elizabeth, 6
Simon, 4, 37, 39
IRONS ADDITION, 4
ISLAND, 51

-J-
JACKSON, Richard, 34
JACOBS, Albart, 27
Albert, 46
Henry, 13
Martha, 46
JACOBSSON, Henry, 14
JACOCKS, William, 40
JAMES, Daniel, 30
Daniell, 4
Richard, 20
JAMES' CHOICE, 4
JAMES VALLEY, 4
JANKINS, Ja., 58
JAQUETT, John, 12
Peter, 12
JARRET, Abraham, 22
JARVIS, Thomas, 4
JENNINGS, John, 28
Sa:, 58
JERMAN, William, 8
JESSOP, Jasper, 22
JESSUP, Jasper, 36
JOHASON, John, 48
JOHN MILLS, 2
JOHNSON, Adam, 28, 46
Adrian, 13

Aron, 15
Charles, 29
Corn:, 52
Cornelius, 8
Francis, 28
H., 31
Henry, 31, 32
James, 26, 58
Robert, 8
Sybrant, 12
Walter, 42
JONES, D., 37
Daniel, 22, 26, 32, 37
Ev., 40
Evan, 4, 41, 43
Gabriel, 22, 28
Gabriell, 25
Gr., 35
Griff, 41
Griff., 35
Griffith, 21
John, 28, 45, 53
Lancelot, 20
Richard, 26
St., 35, 37, 38
Thomas, 16, 27, 49
Walter, 20
JOYCE, Thomas, 25, 59
JOYNING, Galloway, 40
JULOUS, Arthur, 8

-K-
KEARLE, Thomas, 29
KELLEY, John, 21
KELLY, John, 4, 40
Thomas, 57
Timothy, 12
KENNY, William, 8
KERK, John, 8, 55
KETTLE, Cornelius, 11
KICKIN, 46
KICKIN AND KICK-OUT, 46
KICKOUT, 8, 46
KILLINGSWORTH, Edward, 25
KILLINGTON, 4

KING, Bartholomew, 17
 John, 4, 39, 49
 Peter, 17
KINGSDALE, 6
KINGSTON, 5, 59
KIPHAVEN, John, 8
KIPSHAVEN, John, 46, 48
 Martha, 46
KNECKINTON, 3
KOLLUCK, Jacob, 48

-L-
LADYES DELIGHT, 7
LAKE, Daniell, 8
LAMB, George, 10
LAMBOURNE, 1
LAND, Edward, 12
 Francis, 13
LANE, John, 22
 Thomas, 42
LANGSHAW, Thomas, 10
LATHAM, John, 14
LAW, Richard, 27
LAWES, Richard, 8
LAWES CHANCE, 8
LAWRENCE, Hybert, 11, 17
 William, 23, 35
LAWS, Richard, 18
LAWSON, Richard, 49
LEADERNOCK, 6
LEBANON, 9
LEMEN, Henry, 12
LESTER, George, 16
 William, 16
LETTS, Francis, 18
LEVERPOOL, 6
LEVICK, Richard, 4, 37, 41
LEWDEN, Roger, 12
LEWIS, Peter, 26, 47, 48
LILLINGTON,
' Edward, 10, 19
LILLY, Ja:, 57
LINCOLNE, 6

LINFALL, J., 40
LISBON, 1
LISON, Edward, 10
LISTON, Morris, 18
LITTLE BOLTON, 7
LITTLE STRAT-FORD, 9
LITTLEFIELD, More., 53
LOCKIER, Nicholas, 12
LODOWICK HALL, 39
LONDON, 37
LONG, Edward, 16
LONG NECK, 50
LONG REACH, 38
LONGACRE, 1
LONGBEACH, 10
LONGFIELD, 6
LONGFORD, 5
LOOBER, Peter, 23
LOPER, Mich., 31
 Michael, 32
 Peter, 32
LOTT, Engelbert, 10
LOVE, Timothy, 48
LOVELACE, Francis, 42, 45, 55
LOWDE, Edward, 20
LOWE, John, 60
LOWING, N., 49
LOWTHER, Edward, 42
 Susannah, 42
LUFF, Hugh, 24
LUFFE, Adam, 30
 Hugh, 30
LUFT, Hugh, 4
LUSHAM, 3

-M-
MACKARTY, Daniel, 18
 John, 18
MACKDANIELL, John, 20
MACKDONNELL, Bryan, 14

MCKETERICK, John, 40
MAHON, John, 57
 Thomas, 38
MAKINS, Richard, 21
MAKITT, Widow, 25
MALSON, Matthias, 12
MAN., John, 57
MANHON, John, 29
MANKIN, Richard, 15
MANLOE, George, 24, 30
 H. Mol., 30
 John, 29
 Jonathan, 30
 Luke, 25
 Mark, 24
 Thomas, 28
 William, 24, 26
MANLOE'S BOUNDS, 30
MANLOES BOUNDS, 4
MANLOVE, John, 58
 Mark, 57
 Richard, 57
 Thomas, 60
MANLOVE'S GREEN, 30
MANLOW, John, 4
MANSLOW, 4
MARCILLATT, Simon, 12
MARKHAM, William, 30
MARONEY, John, 25
MARRINER, George, 51
MARSH, 8, 56, 61
 James, 48
 Paul, 48
MARTIN, George, 4, 20, 43
 Jeffery, 10
 Martha, 12
MASON, Matthew, 40
MATSON, John, 12
MATTHEWS, Oliver, 13

Thomas, 13
MAURIS, Jacob, 31
MAXFIELD, James, 4
MAXFIELDS, John, 29
MAXWELL, James, 22, 38
Robert, 38
MAY, Margaret, 57
T., 58
Thomas, 29, 57, 58
MAYDSTON, 1
MAYNER, Joseph, 28
MAYS, 59
MELLANY, Timothy, 13
MESTON, Arthur, 22, 36, 37, 40
METCALFE, Thomas, 13
MICHAEL, Otto, 11, 17
MICHELTOWNE, 2
MICKLE, Archbd., 60
MIDDLEBOROUGH, 1
MIDDLETON, George, 8
MIDDLETOWNE, 1
MIDGELY, Thomas, 28
MIERS, John, 28
MILBOURNE, 7
MILL LAND, 33
MILL, PLANTATION, THE, 53
MILLAR, Esther, 34
Reb., 34
MILLER, Andrew, 22
James, 19
Solomon, 37
Thomas, 24
MILLINGTON, John, 51
MILLNER, William, 29
MILLS, John, 4, 5, 25
MILNOR, William, 57
MIRES, John, 57
MITCHEL, 44
Richard, 31, 32

MITCHELL, Richard, 43
MOLESTEDY, Al., 49
Alexander, 47
MOLESTINE, Abraham, 48
Al:, 48
Alex, 46
Alexander, 46, 47
MOLESTON, Abraham, 28
Thomas, 29
MOLINE, Peter, 13
MOLL, John, 17
MOLLESTINE, Henry, 30
MOLLESTON, Henry, 30, 58
MOLSTON, Thomas, 53
Will, 53
MONS, Peter, 16
MOOR, George, 11
Joseph, 11, 14
MOORE, Christopher, 4
Joseph, 4
MORGAN, David, 34, 35
George, 22, 35, 36
Henry, 20
Jamima, 46
John, 34, 46
Matthew, 35
MORLATTO HALL, 8
MORPHEY, Philomy, 14
MORRIS, James, 44
John, 45
MORSLEY, Will, 29
MORTON, William, 21, 31, 32, 35, 36, 37, 41
MOTHER PLANTATION, 3
MOTLOW, 4
MOTT, S., 33
Samuel, 4
MOULESTON, Alexander, 8

MOULISTON, Alexander, 27
MOUNSON, Peter, 15
MOUNT, (THE), 4, 6
MUDDY BRANCH WHEEL OF FORTUNE, 40
MUMFORD, John, 1
MURDOCK, Robert, 52
MURPHY, Charles, 4
Nicholas, 43
MURROUGH, Richard, 25
MUSMELLON, 40

-N-
NACARROE, John, 20
NECARROW, John, 41
NEEDHAM, ---, 21
Edmond, 24, 35
Ezekiel, 35
NEW DESIGN, 35
NEWALL, John, 5
NEWCOMB, Bapt., 50, 52, 53, 54, 59
Baptis, 29
Baptist, 8
Bapts, 5
NEWCOME, Baptist, 52
Daniel, 52
William, 52
William Baptist, 52
NEWCOMS BURROW, 8
NEWELL, John, 32
NEWINGTON, 5
NEWTON, Edward, 5
NICHOLS, John, 34
Thomas, 24
NICHOLSON, John, 36
NICKOLLS, Robert, 24
William, 24
NIXON, Thomas, 8, 16
NOBLE, Richard, 5, 37, 55

NOMERS, John, 14
NONSUCH, 8
NORTH HARTFORD, 8
NORTHAMPTON, 35, 44
NUTTER, John, 57

-O-
OAKEY, John, 28
OALSON, Henry, 17
Peter, 17
O'DONOHOE, Michael, 32
OGLE, John, 14
Thomas, 14
OKEY, John, 8
OLDMAN, Thomas, 28
O'NEALE, Brian, 5
OSBORN, Mathew, 8
OSBORNE, Matthew, 29
OSBOURN, William, 18
OTTERHAVEN, Leonard, 10
OWEN, Lewis, 18
William, 26

-P-
PACKE, Alice, 5
Edward, 5
PAGE, Edward, 29
Thomas, 29
PAINTER, John, 48, 49
Richard, 29, 45, 49
PALMETARY, Robert, 20, 21
PALMITARY, Robert, 42
PALMONTARY, Robert, 5
PARADEE, Stephen, 37
PARINGTON, 5
PARKER, ---, 14
Anderson, 48
Laurence, 19

Will, 29
PARLING, Simon, 29
PARMAIN, Henry, 43
PARRY, Rowld:, 54, 55
William, 23
PARSLEY, Anthony, 8, 29
PARTNERSHIP, 3
PARTTY, Richard, 8
PARVIS, Robert, 5
PASHALIA, 8
PASTURE POINT, 2
PASTURE POYNT, 9
PATRICK, Roger, 5
PATTISON, William, 17
PATTY, John, 53
Richard, 53
PAYNTER, Richard, 51
Sarah, 51
PAYREMAINE, Henry, 20
PEACH BLOSSOM, 49
PEALY, Richard, 52
PEARSON, John, 18
Thomas, 13
PECK, William, 58
PEDDINGTON, Henry, 8
PEMBERTON, Thomas, 5, 27, 30, 43, 51
PENN, William, 48
PENNINGTON, Henry, 58, 60
John, 13
PENSEY, 7
PERDRIO, Peter, 10
PERDUE, Stephen, 37
PETERKIN, James, 28, 45
PETERS BERRY, 9
PETERSBOROUGH, 5
PETERSON, Adam, 18, 19
Hans, 15

Paul, 15
Peter, 16
Thomas, 5
Widdow, 15
PETIT, Abrah: Clement, 54
PETTYJOHN, John, 28, 47
PEWS HILL, 9
PEY, John, 29
PHARSALIA PLAINS, 5
PHILIPS, Frederick, 34
PHILLIPS, Frederick, 1
PICKERING, Charles, 5
PICKWICK, 9
PILES, W., 55
William, 27, 52, 55, 56
PILTON, 38
PINER, Edward, 5
PIPE ELM, 6
PITTS, John, 28
PLAINS OF JERICHO, 5
PLAYNER, William, 8
PLEASANT, 7
PLEASANT FARMS, 8
POINT LOOKOUT, 2, 3, 9
POOLE, William, 16
POPLAR RIDGE, 1, 36
PORTER, Law., 40
Robert, 21, 40
POTTER, Ab:, 52
Abr., 51, 52, 54
Abr:, 51
Abraham, 8, 53
James, 40
Jane, 52, 53
POULSON, Peter, 14
POWEL, Daniel, 30
POWLSON, Olle, 13
PRESTON, S., 60
Samuel, 30, 45, 46
Samuell, 27

PRETTIMAN, John, 45
PRETTYMAN, John, 46, 51
PREW, John, 16
PRICE, John, 5
Nicholas Daniel, 11
Thomas, 5
PRICE'S CHOICE, 4
PRICES HAVEN, 8
PRIME, Ralph, 43
PROVOOST, Johannes, 31
PUCKLE, N., 56

-R-
RAKESTRAW, William, 14
RANGE, THE, 39
RANGLINTON, 8
RAWLINS, John, 5
RAWSON, Olle, 16
RAYMAN, Peter, 48
RAYMON, Peter, 26
READ, George, 14
James, 11
REHOBOA, 46
REHOBOA PEACH BLOSSOM, 49
REHOBOA YOUNG'S HOPE, 49
RENNOLDS, Richard, 29
RENOLDS, Francis, 33
RESERVE, THE, 5
REYNOLDS, Henry, 16
John, 11, 14, 31, 42, 43
Joseph, 42
Mary, 31
Richard, 12, 57
Thomas, 43
William, 42, 44
RICH FARME, 9
RICH PASTURE, 5
RICHARDS, Grace, 56
John, 27, 29, 53, 55, 56, 58, 60
Robert, 51

William, 53
RICHARDS PUR-CHASE, 56
RICHARDSON, 38
Daniel, 14
David, 12
Francis, 31, 32
J., 41
John, 5, 6, 15, 21, 35, 36, 39, 40, 41
Parnell, 21, 25
William, 38
RICHARDSON'S, 41
RICHARDSONS, Francis, 49
RICHMORE, 6
RIDNY, John, 31
RINIER, 3
ROAD PLANTA-TION, 9
ROADES, John, 5, 9, 48
ROBERT'S CHANCE, 42
ROBERTSBURY, 5
ROBINSON, George, 24, 31
John, 5, 23
Robert, 15
Widow, 14
ROBISON, George, 16
John, 33
William, 15
ROBISSON, Patrick, 56
ROCHESTER, 1
ROCK, Owen, 48
ROD, John, 31
Will, 31
RODENEY, John, 31
Will, 5
William, 23, 38
RODENY, Capt., 36
W., 32, 41
William, 32, 35, 37, 38
RODNEY STOCK, 1
ROTHWELL, Thomas, 17
ROUSE, Thomas, 23
ROWE, John, 53
ROWLAND, S., 45

Samuel, 45, 54, 55, 62
ROWLD, Sa:, 45
ROWLES, B., 55
Bryan, 55
Bryant, 27
RUDE, John, 23
RUMSY, Charles, 13
John, 13
RUSSAEL, Philip, 29
RUTTINGTON, 5
RUTTY, Daniel, 5, 31, 32, 34
Eleanor, 34
RYE, John, 8

-S-
SAHAWN, Samuel
Thomas, 41
ST. CULLOMB, 1
ST. MARTIN, 46
SAMPLE, Widdow, 6
SANDIDGE, John, 18
SARDYNE, Johannes, 11
SAVAGE, John, 9
SAWMILL RANGE, 1
SAWYER, Thomas, 14
SCARFE, William, 18
SCOTT, Comfort, 26
Elias, 11
Jeremy, 9
SEATON, 4
James, 60
SEKS, Nathaniel, 28
SELBY, Thomas, 5
SELOOVER, Isaac, 11
SELYNS, Henry, 31
Mary, 31
SHACKBURY, John, 51
SHAKLEY, James, 6
SHANKLAND, William, 46
SHARNES, William, 6
SHARP, George, 21
John, 5
Thomas, 21, 39, 43, 44
SHARPBURN, 5
SHARPE, John, 5
SHAW, Richard, 28
Thomas, 22

SHEARLY, John, 24
SHEARNESS, 1
SHELLAWAY, 9
SHEPARD, John, 23
SHEPERD, Hercules, 27
SHEPPARD, George, 5
  John, 34, 51
SHERER, William, 43
SHERRER, William, 20
SHERRY, Margaret, 10
SHERWOOD, William, 43, 44
SHERWOOD'S FORTUNE, 43
SHERWOOD'S PURCHASE, 6
SHICKBURY, John, 51
SHIPTON, 2
SHIRE, Thomas, 29
SHOEMAKER'S HALL, 33
SHORE, William, 6
SHORT, Adam, 12
SHOULDER, Richard, 9, 50
SHREWSBERRY, 41
SHREWSBURY, 41
SIDBOTTOM, Robert, 24
SIKES, Thomas, 29
SIMON, Frances, 6
  John, 49
SIMONDS, William, 9
SIMONS, Hugh, 14
  Stephen, 23
  William, 27
SIMSON CHOICE, 40
SIMSON'S CHOICE, 40, 41
SINEX, Broer, 15
SINKIS, Michael, 39
SIPPLE, Garret, 34
SITTINGBURN, 3
SITTINGBURNE, 5

SKARBORROUGH, 5
SKIDMORE, 5, 60
  Henry, 9
  Joseph, 32, 38
  Th., 58, 60
  Thomas, 5, 23, 24, 25, 34
SLAUGHTER, John, 38
SMIRNA, 2
SMITH, Anthony, 17
  Daniel, 35
  Francis, 15
  Gerhard, 12
  Henry, 9, 55, 59
  Jacob, 22
  Jenkins, 29
  John, 9, 13, 22, 34, 37, 59
  Maurice, 37
  Robert, 40
  Thomas, 50
SOTTER, Abraham, 28
SOUTHBE, William, 44
SOUTHERON, Edward, 46
SPENCER, Frances, 60, 61
  Henry, 28, 61
  Samuel, 61
  William, 5, 9, 57, 58, 61
SPENCERS HALL, 57
SPICER, William, 48
SPOONER, Charles, 9, 29
SPOONERS CORNER, 7
SPOONERS HALL, 9
SPRINGER, Charles, 13
SPRINGFIELD, 2
STALCUP, Peter, 15
  Widow, 13
STANDLEY, Christopher, 21

STAPLEFORD, Thomas, 58, 60
STAPLETON, Will, 29
  William, 58, 60
STAR, Richard, 29
STARKEY, Edward, 21
STARR, N., 53
  Nathaniel, 53, 54
STEEDHAM, Erasmus, 13
  Lucas, 15
  Lulif, 15
STEEL, James, 44
STEELE, James, 44
STEENWICK, Cornelius, 31
STEPHENS, Matthew, 27
STEVENS, Henry, 36
  John, 37
  William, 38, 41
STEVENSON, Henry, 5
STEWART, John, 47
STOCKLY, Charles, 28
  John, 27
  Woodman, 27
STOLL, Joost, 15
STONE, Basil, 19
  Isaac, 21
STONES, James, 24
STRATFORD, 9
STRATHAM, 2
STRATTON, Thomas, 5
STREAT, John, 51
STREATE, John, 28
STREET, John, 9, 51, 52, 53
STRETCHER, Henry, 26, 51, 54
STRETCHERS HALL, 7
STULERANT, Turlus, 19
STURGES, Elizabeth, 49
  John, 9

Jonathan, 49
SWAM, Elizabeth, 34
Richard, 34
SWAMPBOURNE, 2
SWAN POINT, 55
SWEATMAN,
William, 48, 49
SWETMAN, William,
26
SWINFORD, 39
SYBRANT, John, 12
SYKES, James, 56
John, 18
Nathaniel, 56
SYMONDS, William,
50, 52
SYPRES HALL, 7

-T-
TANTON, 5
TAYLOR, John, 18
Katherin, 9
TENDERITH, 3
TEYNEDS COURT, 3
THOMAS, 57
Gabr:, 56
James, 42
Olle, 14
William, 29, 42
THOMPSON, Jethro,
20, 43
THOMSON, Jeffry, 6
Jethro, 43
Mary, 40
Urba:, 40
THORRD, T., 35
THORROLD,
Timothy, 35
TIDBURY, 3
TILTON, Thomas, 9,
27, 57, 61
TIMBERNECK, 9
TIVERTON, 37
TOAES, Daniel, 35, 39
TOARSON, Henry, 16
John, 16
TOBIAS, James, 40
TOBISSON, Dennis,
21
TOM, William, 45

TOMLINSON,
Robert, 27
TOMMAS, William, 23
TOMPSON, Vebanus,
21
TOPSHAM, 1
TORNSON, William,
12
TOWNSEND, John,
23, 33, 34
TRIANGLE, THE, 1
TRIBET, William, 6
TRIPINGTON, 6
TRIPPET, William,
31, 32
TRIPPINGTON, 32
TROTTER, William,
47
TURBURY, John, 27
TURNER, ---, 43
Annanias, 24
Elizabeth, 34
Richard, 20, 43
TWILLEY, George, 25
TWILLINGTON, 9
TWILLY, Robert, 9

-U-
UNDERWOOD,
Samuell, 15
URINSON, Christian,
13
Henry, 15
USBAND, John, 28

-V-
VALE, THE VALE
OF FOUNTAIN, 6
VANDERBURGH,
Henry, 11
VANDERENLINE,
Reynier, 11
Zecheriah, 11
VANDERHEYDEN,
Matthias, 10
VANDERVEER,
Jacob, 15
John, 15
William, 15
VANGEZELL, Jacob,
11

VANGODEN, John,
31
VANKERK, Rowly, 8
VANKIRK, Art
Johnson, 27
Arthur Johnson, 8
VANS, John, 15
VAUGHAN, David,
13
VERHOOF, Corn, 6
Corn:, 53, 55, 56
Cornelius, 3, 9, 31, 49
VERHOOFE, Corn.,
50
VERKIRK, Art, 58, 60
VICKERIDGE, Isaac,
18
VICKORY, John, 6
VINES, John, 9, 49,
58, 60
VINEYARD, THE, 3

-W-
WADDLE, Thomas,
22
WALKER, Ja., 48
James, 46
John, 3, 24, 26, 39, 48
Nath:, 54
Nathaniel, 10, 50
Richard, 6
Thomas, 6
WALL, Richard, 33
WALLOWE, Henry,
60
WALLS, Richard, 24,
34
WALRAVEN,
Gisbert, 15
Henry, 17
Jonas, 15
WALTHAM, John,
58, 60
WALTON, Michael,
23
Nicholas, 35
WAPLE, W., 51
WAPLES, Peter, 27
WARD, Richard, 28
WARGENT, William,
59

WARING, Jacob, 27
WARREN, Jacob, 52
WASHINGTON,
John, 19
WASTECOAT,
Josiah, 47
Mary, 47
WATON, 8
WATSON, Isaac, 56,
57
John, 9, 56, 59
L., 57, 61
Luke, 6, 9, 29, 45, 47,
56, 57
Samuel, 9, 56
Samuell, 29
Sarah, 47
WATSONS MAR-
SHES, 9
WATSON'S PUR-
CHASE, 45
WATTS, John, 11
WATTSON, John, 28
WEBB, H., 33
Robert, 32
WEBLY, 46
WEDMORE, 38
WELBOURNE,
Thomas, 9
WELLS, 5
Ja:, 49
James, 6, 39, 41, 50
Thomas, 34
WEST, Elizabeth, 48
John, 48
Josia, 27
Thomas, 28
WESTINGDALE,
Percifull, 18
WESTMORELAND,
6, 43
WETFOODT,
Francis, 44
WETSWORTH,
Francis, 18
WHEATFIELD, 2
WHEEL OF FOR-
TUNE, 40
WHEELDON, Isaac,
19

WHEELER, John, 58,
59
WHEELERS HALL, 8
WHETMAN, ---, 29
WHIT, William, 29
WHITE, Christopher,
14
John, 11
Rickson, 9
William, 45
WHITE HORSE, 8
WHITEHALL, 3, 9,
42, 43
Richard, 7
WHITESIDE,
George, 15
WHITTMAN,
Stephan, 10
WHITWELL, Francis,
5, 6, 44
WHITWELLS, 2
WILBANK, Harman, 6
WILLET, William, 9
WILLIAM, Mary, 11
WILLIAM AND
THOMAS, THE 6
WILLIAMS,
Alexander, 6
Edward, 9, 28
Francis, 9, 28
George, 17
Henry, 10
James, 18
John, 10, 28, 29, 47, 50
Reynier, 24
Richard, 6, 9, 24, 54
Rinier, 6
Thomas, 6, 24, 58, 60
William, 6
WILLINGBROOK, 39
WILLSON, Abell, 22
John, 21
Matthew, 22
Richard, 21, 24
Thomas, 22, 29
William, 20
WILSON, Abel, 36
Elizabeth, 40
James, 28
John, 18

Matthew, 36
R., 42
Reb., 36
Richard, 6, 40
Thomas, 6, 21, 36, 60
Widow, 39
William, 6
WILTBANK, Abrah.,
62
Abraham, 50
Corn., 62
Cornelius, 26, 61
Her. Fred., 55
Herm:, 50
Herm: Fred:, 45
Hermannus, 61
Hermanus, 62
Isaac, 45, 62
John, 50
WINDER, John, 54, 61
WINSMORE, Mary,
36
William, 6, 22, 36
WINSMORES
DALE, 6
WOLF, William, 53
WOLLASTON,
Thomas, 14
WOOD, Patrick, 40
WOODBERRY, 8
WOODFORD, 3
WOODLAND, Wil-
liam, 17
WOODS, Anthony, 14
Thomas, 28
WOODSTOCK
CORNER, 4
WOOLBANK, Hal-
manus, 10
WOOLFE, William, 29
WOOLGAST, Arthur,
10
WOOTEON, John, 59
WORD, Patrick, 6
WORMINGHURST,
59
WOTTON, Roger, 11
WRIGHT, Aminadab,
6
Charles, 28

WYNNE, Elizabeth, 51
  J., 45
  Jonathan, 28, 45
  Margery, 51
  Thomas, 45, 51, 60
  Widow, 26

  -Y-
YE LONG REACH,
35
YE POINT, 61
YONG, George, 10
YORK, N., 58
YOUNG, George, 49
  John, 47

.

www.ingramcontent.com/pod-product-compliance
Lightning Source LLC
LaVergne TN
LVHW051706080426
835511LV00017B/2749